EXPLORING AUSTRALIA'S

GREAT
BARRIER REEF

A WORLD HERITAGE SITE

EXPLORING AUSTRALIA'S

GREAT BARRIER REEF

A WORLD HERITAGE SITE

LESTER CANNON
AND
MARK GOYEN

The Watermark Press

CONTRIBUTORS AND CONSULTANTS

DR LESTER R. G. CANNON
Senior Curator, Lower Invertebrates
Queensland Museum

DR MARK GOYEN
Photographer and writer
Sydney

PROFESSOR DAVID HOPLEY
Head of Sir George Fisher Centre for Tropical Marine Studies
James Cook University of North Queensland

RON COLEMAN
Curator of Maritime History and Archaeology
Queensland Museum

PROFESSOR HAROLD HEATWOLE
Department of Zoology
The University of New England

LESLEY HOWARD MURDOCH
Education Information Officer
Great Barrier Reef Marine Park Authority

CALVIN TILLEY
North Queensland Sport and Game Fishing Services

RAY NEALE
Assistant Executive Officer
Great Barrier Reef Marine Park Authority

PHOTOGRAPHS

Rob Adlard: 28, 82, 83. Ron Coleman: 50, 52, 54 top, 56, 57 top, 58 top, 60 bottom right. Ben Cropp/Auscape: 127 top. Mark Goyen: 9, 11, 17, 18, 19, 20, 23, 26, 29, 31, 61, 62, 63, 64, 65, 66, 67, 68, 69, 70, 71, 72, 73, 74, 75, 76, 77, 78, 79, 80, 86, 87, 88, 89, 90, 91, 92, 93, 94, 95, 96, 97, 98, 99, 100, 101, 103, 104, 105, 106, 107, 108, 109, 110, 111, 113, 114, 115, 116, 117, 118, 120, 121, 122, 123, 124, 125, 128, 129, 130, 134, 135, 136, 137, 138, 139, 140, 141, 142, 143, 144, 145, 146, 147, 148, 149, 150, 151, 182, 183, 184, 186, 187, 188, 189, 190, 191, 192, 193, 200, 201, 202, 203, 204, 205, 206, 207, 208, 209, 213, 214, 215. Harold Heatwole: 152, 153, 158, 159, 160, 161, 162, 163, 164, 165, 167, 168, 169, 170, 171, 173, 174, 175, 177, 179, 180, 181. David Hopley: 18, 21, 22, 24, 25, 27, 34, 35, 38, 39, 40, 41, 42, 43. Ross Isaacs: 132, 133. John Mondora: 216, 218. Leslie Newman: 84, 85. Parer-Cook/Auscape: 127 bottom.

Maps — Great Barrier Reef Marine Park Authority: 12. Sophie Blackall: 194, 196, 198.

Pictures courtesy of — Alan Bond: 47 top. Mitchell Library, NSW: 44, 47 bottom. Queensland Museum: 49, 50 bottom, 53, 54, 57 bottom, 58 bottom, 59, 60 top, 166. Great Barrier Reef Marine Park Authority: 102.

A WATERMARK PRESS BOOK

EXPLORING AUSTRALIA'S GREAT BARRIER REEF
was created and produced by
The Watermark Press,
Australia.

Project Editor	Simon Blackall
Editors	Kate Foord
	Tania Hackett
	Camilla Sandell
Designer	Susan Kinealy
Production	James Somerled
	Claude Parsons

National Library of Australia
Cataloguing-in-Publication Data.

Cannon, L. R. G. (Lester Robert Glen), 1940–
Exploring Australia's Great Barrier Reef

Includes index.
ISBN 0 949284 15 7

1. Great Barrier Reef (Qld.) — Description and travel —
Guide-books. I Goyen, Mark. II Title.

919.43'0463

Typeset by Saba Graphics Ltd, New Zealand.
Produced by Mandarin Offset, Hong Kong.

CONTENTS

Masthead Island. A typical forested coral cay, one of the larger islands in the Capricorn group.

INTRODUCTION

L E S T E R C A N N O N

THE Great Barrier Reef region stretches for over 2000 km along the coast of Queensland, from just north of Fraser Island in the south (24°30°S) to beyond Cape York in the north (10°S). It covers an area of about 350 000 square kilometres on the continental shelf of Australia.

It was Matthew Flinders who coined the term 'Great Barrier Reef' when exploring the coast of North Queensland for a safe shipping passage in 1802. In fact, although it has remained in use, the term is inaccurate. The region, far from being a single entity, consists of nearly 3000 individual coral reefs. Furthermore, the outer reefs do not form an actual barrier, nor make the coastal waters into one immense lagoon. The reefs, however, do divert ocean currents and, in many places, intercept the ocean swell.

Biologically, the Great Barrier Reef represents the most diverse ecosystem known. Because of the extraordinary efficiency of algae and corals in extracting and using nutrients and other materials from a nutrient-poor sea, the ecosystem is a highly productive one. The Reef's tropical waters are inhabited by animals and plants with the ability to produce substantial formations of calcium carbonate. This results in the maintenance and growth of the Great Barrier Reef, the world's largest single collection of coral reefs. There are over 340 species of reef forming hard corals on the Great Barrier Reef and a further 60 species of soft corals.

Coral reefs have successfully developed in shallow seas for over 500 million years. Originally reefs were built by the now extinct rugose corals, but about 200 million years ago scleractinian corals, similar to those found today, became the dominant forms. By 100 million years ago, these had developed extensively in the Tethys Sea, a huge ocean of water that lay between the land masses of northern Europe and Asia and the continents of southern Africa and India. With the process of continental drift the Tethys Sea was closed off. The southern continents began to move northwards and the distribution of corals gradually extended eastwards. In the warm tropical waters of the western Pacific extensive reef formation began about 40 to 50 million years ago. Today over 500 species of corals can be found in these waters, making them the site of the world's most diverse range of corals.

The Australian continent also began its drift northward at this time away from the cold, polar region into the warmer, tropical waters. The Great Barrier Reef is therefore, at most, 18 million years old and in some places only two million years old; remarkably young considering how long coral reefs have existed.

During this time the Reef, like many other reefs, has survived dramatic changes in the environment. Large variations in sea level have occurred — to 150 metres below the present level, and also some metres above it. For the last 6000 years the sea level has remained fairly constant and as a consequence today's living reef is only a few thousand years old. The earliest evidence of new growth since the last major rise in sea level dates back only 8000 years.

The fundamental unit of the coral reef is the coral polyp. Corals can reproduce both asexually by budding and sexually. The young are free-swimming larvae or planulae which, once they find a suitable place to settle, will metamorphose, i.e. change their form dramatically. Each begins to feed via a tentacle-fringed mouth and also to lay down a limestone base and to form a skeleton. In soft corals this skeleton is merely a collection of splinters (spicules) which may form a central chalky column encased in the body. In hard or true corals the polyp builds a skeleton from below and can draw itself inside for protection.

It is only in warm waters where the average temperature does not fall below 18°C that polyps will be reef builders. As the majority of reef corals reproduce asexually by budding, whole colonies grow gradually upwards and outwards. Upward growth ceases when a coral reaches sea level; outward growth is often limited by competition for space with other corals.

It was Charles Darwin who, in 1842, first developed a system of classification for coral reefs, describing fringing reefs, barrier reefs and open ocean atolls. Fringing reefs occur in shallow seas next to islands or continents. Further offshore barrier reefs are found, separated from the mainland by shallow seas. Atolls form in deeper oceans, usually over volcanic foundations which are later submerged. This creates a central lagoon with the coral formed around it.

Fringing reefs occur off the coast of 540 of the Great Barrier Reef's high continental islands. On the windward side of these islands, because of the effects of strong south-easterly trade winds, corals have little chance to develop and usually form narrow ledges no wider than 20 metres. On the protected leeward side, however, reef flats of over one kilometre are quite common.

The Great Barrier Reef varies considerably along its length. In the north there is a maze of *wall* or *ribbon* reefs separated by channels generally narrower than 1000 metres. The ribbons are usually no more than 500 metres wide, but can be up to 25 kilometres long, and form parallel to the continental shelf. *Platform* or *patch* reefs form inside the ribbon reefs. They are large and flat, oval-shaped, and can be up to 25 kilometres long. Much of the mainland, with its shallow waters, has *fringing* reefs.

The central region is composed mainly of patch reefs. Here the continental shelf widens considerably and the Great Barrier Reef is confined largely to the outer sea. Fringing reefs border the numerous islands between Cairns and Mackay.

The reefs of this central region are considerably younger than those of the northern and southern regions. The present-day sea level was reached by the reefs in this region only 3000 years ago, some 3000 years after the areas to the north and south. Consequently, there are fewer reefs, and the reef flats are lower and smaller.

In the south, the Reef is characterised by deeper shelf waters, far fewer mainland fringing reefs, and most of the reefs are separated from the mainland by a very wide body of comparatively deep water. The outer reefs of this sector extend from the Pompey Reefs in the north to the Swain Reefs in the south. The Swain Reefs are, at the closest, 150 kilometres from the mainland, and across this expanse lies the Capricorn Channel. The area is one of the most spectacular of the Great Barrier Reef — the reefs are large and intricate, divided by narrow channels which form complex systems resembling the delta of a large river. Where the Pompey Reefs join the Swain Reefs is a network of lagoons and mid-reef coral ridges, the lagoons deepening towards the south of the complex.

The inner reefs of this southern section experience the highest tidal ranges of any of the world's coral reefs. This range, between five and six metres, has resulted in the formation of terraced platforms which in turn means that, at low tide, lagoons can be isolated almost three metres above the surrounding ocean.

South and landwards of the Swain Reefs are the Bunker and Capricorn groups, comprising 22 emergent reefs, many with vegetated cays, and 11 shoals. Here, in the southernmost region of the Great Barrier Reef, the continental shelf is little more than 90 kilometres wide. The reefs in this area, particularly towards the centre, tend to be small with enclosed lagoons.

A majestic fish, aptly named, is the magnificently coloured emperor angel fish, *Pomacanthus imperator*.

The Great Barrier Reef is one of the seven wonders of the natural world. It is a system of extraordinary biological complexity, of superb ecological balance. Each area of the Reef performs a vital role in its maintenance and growth — food must be provided, waste consumed, nutrients recycled, and the Reef's limestone base must be maintained and continue to grow.

Reefs provide their own food supply in a constant process of recycling, which means that they can survive in the most barren areas. The near absence of plant nutrients in tropical seas means that there is little plankton growth, and this results in the spectacular blue that characterises these waters. In areas of more abundance coral reefs tend not to be able to compete with other marine systems. Reefs, however, are not confined solely to these nutrient-poor areas, but can be found in a number of different marine environments.

Surprisingly, only a small proportion of the corals' food and energy comes from feeding on reef plankton. Most is obtained from *zooxanthellae*, the minute algae existing within the coral tissues. Even though they are animals, corals really function chiefly as plants. Sunlight provides the basic energy for the production of food, and reef systems are maintained and continue to grow because of the photosynthetic activities of the coral's algal symbionts. For photosynthesis to occur light penetration must be high, and the water cannot be deep or turbid. It is unlikely that reefs would form below about 50 metres.

The formation of a reef requires great amounts of calcium which, along with carbon dioxide, is plentiful in sea water. Elements such as nitrogen and phosphorus, and any other trace elements needed, are recycled, being unavailable in large enough quantities. Blue-green algae perform an important role in this process, as they produce soluble inorganic nitrogen nutrients by converting amospheric nitrogen gas.

Photosynthesis accounts for the use of approximately 75 per cent of the carbon dioxide extracted from reef waters. Over each 24-hour period this process creates between 20 and 50 grams per square metre of new organic matter. This constitutes the major source of food, as it is consumed almost entirely by the reef, moves through the food chain, and returns eventually to the water as carbon dioxide.

The 25 per cent of carbon dioxide not used in the creation of new organic matter goes directly to creating the reef structure, by being used in the formation of calcium carbonate or limestone.

The intensity of biological activity within a reef is not uniform. Some parts will be far more active than others. The most productive area, in which the highest level of photosynthesis and limestone formation occurs, is the upper section of the seaward reef slopes. This area is also a source zone, as organic matter which breaks off here is transported to other, less active, parts of the reef, particularly the backreef or lagoon.

The highest physical energy received by the reef occurs in the outer parts of the reef flat, as these areas are the most exposed to waves and storms. The biological activity is therefore less intense. The central part of the reef flat is less susceptible to such influences, and levels of photosynthesis and calcium carbonate formation are much higher. In this area the reef is basically self-sufficient, consuming most of the food produced. Further upward growth is prevented because the reef flat is really at the low-tide sea level.

Aside from the coral, the Great Barrier Reef is probably best-known for its spectacular variety of fishes. Over 1500 species, from coral trout and sweetlips to marlin can be found in Reef waters. The range of sizes, shapes and colours combine with the overwhelming beauty of the coral itself to make the Great Barrier Reef one of the world's natural wonders.

The Reef is also home to a bewildering array of invertebrates, including molluscs such as trochus and helmet shells, cowries and giant clams; echinoderms, among them the infamous crown of thorns starfish, crustaceans, many a gourmet's delight, worms and ascidians.

Delicate fin folds clothe deadly spines: the lion fish (*Pterois volitans*).

Nudibranchs, shell-less snails, are among the most beautiful of reef creatures (*Ardeodonis egretta*).

THE GREAT BARRIER REEF MARINE PARK AUTHORITY

The 1950s saw the beginnings of an environmental awareness and concern amongst the Australian public about the increasing and potential impacts on the Reef from human activity. In the '60s serious conflict on and about the Reef and its management arose when the people of Australia became aware of, and objected to, proposals to drill for oil and to mine limestone on the Reef. The ensuing controversy revealed that the Reef was treasured by many Australians who believed that its uniqueness, biological diversity, beauty and grandeur should be protected by comprehensive management. Since then, more has been learnt about the effects on the Reef of oil spills and polluted run-off from the mainland.

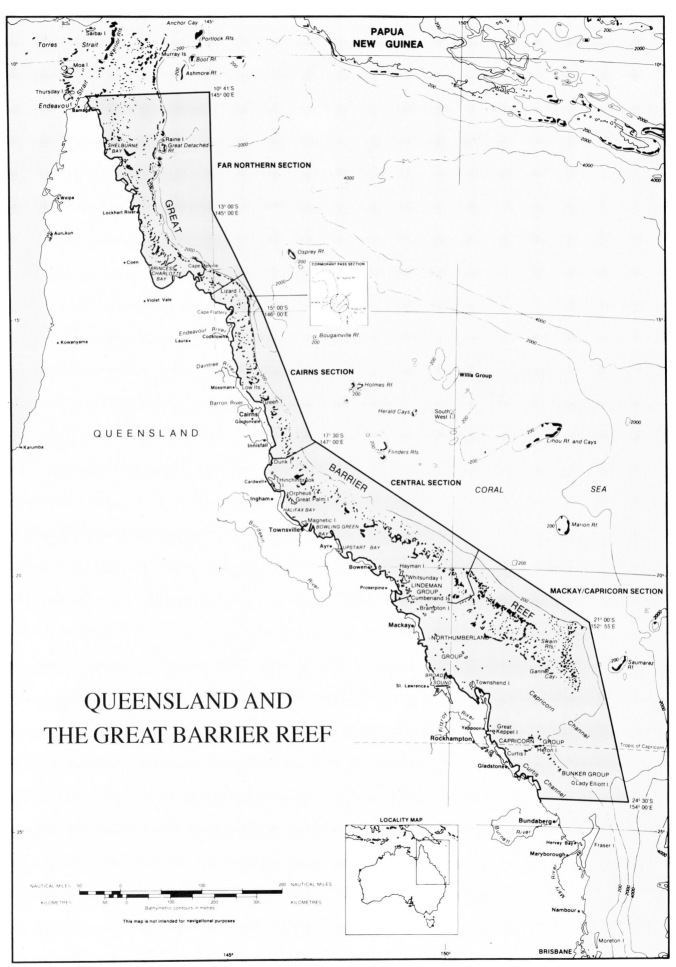

QUEENSLAND AND
THE GREAT BARRIER REEF

This map courtesy of the Great Barrier Reef Marine Park Authority.

The Great Barrier Reef Marine Park Act

The legal basis for protection and management of the Great Barrier Reef was provided by the Great Barrier Reef Marine Park Act which was passed unanimously by both Houses of the Australian Parliament in 1975.

The implementation of the Act involved establishing collaborative arrangements with the Queensland State Government regarding complementary management of islands and intertidal areas of the Great Barrier Reef region which are not within the Great Barrier Reef Marine Park. The Act and the complementary arrangements provided the necessary evidence of appropriate management and support for the World Heritage Committee to list the Reef.

The Great Barrier Reef Marine Park was proclaimed and zoned for management in a number of sections. The first, proclaimed in 1979 represented three and a half per cent of the Great Barrier Reef area. By 1983, the Great Barrier Reef Marine Park had been increased to 348 700 square kilometres, covering 98.5 per cent of the Reef and making it the largest marine park in the world.

The Great Barrier Reef Marine Park Act provides for conservative and reasonable use of the Reef region. The only activity specifically precluded by the Act is the conduct of operations for the recovery of minerals unless for the purpose of research and investigations approved by the Marine Park Authority.

Zoning

The basis for management is provided by zoning plans prepared for four sections. Each zoning plan divides a section into zones and defines the purposes for which each zone may be used or entered. The zoning plans provide for multiple use management. They range from the highly restricted 'preservation zones', which may only be used for the purposes of scientific research that cannot be carried out in any other zone, to the little restricted general use 'A' zones in which a very wide range of activities, including trawling and other forms of commercial fishing may take place. For each zone a plan defines uses to which it may be put, e.g. some may only need prior notification while others may need a permit. The effects are summarised in this Table.

	GENERAL USE 'A' ZONE	GENERAL USE 'B' ZONE	MARINE NATIONAL PARK 'A' ZONE	MARINE NAT PARK BUFFER ZONE	MARINE NATIONAL PARK 'B' ZONE	SCIENTIFIC RESEARCH ZONE	PRESERVATION ZONE
BOATING, DIVING	Yes	Yes	Yes	Yes	Yes	No	No
COLLECTING (e.g. shells, coral, aquarium fish)	Permit	Permit	No	No	No	No	No
LINE FISHING	Yes	Yes	Yes	No	No	No	No
BAIT NETTING	Yes	Yes	Yes	No	No	No	No
TROLLING for pelagic species	Yes	Yes	Yes	Yes	No	No	No
SPEARFISHING (N.B. Not with SCUBA)	Yes	Yes	No	No	No	No	No
POLE & LINE TUNA FISHING	Permit	Permit	No	No	No	No	No
TRAWLING	Yes	No	No	No	No	No	No
CRUISE SHIPS	Yes	Permit	Permit	Permit	Permit	No	No
GENERAL SHIPPING	Yes	No	No	No	No	No	No

The underlying purpose of the zoning plans is to provide for conservation and reasonable use: determination of what is reasonable requires detailed understanding of user and public attitudes as well as scientific understanding of the Reef. The development of zoning plans involves a program with two three-month periods of public participation and ultimate parliamentary approval.

The declared goal of the Authority is 'to provide for the protection, wise use, understanding and enjoyment of the Great Barrier Reef in perpetuity'. This goal, if it is to be achieved, requires that human activities must not be allowed to exceed sustainable levels. No activity can be permitted which stresses the Reef system, or part of it, beyond the recovery rate. This is the same principle that underlies the World Conservation Strategy. The strategic principles used in the management of the Marine Park are those which underlie UNESCO's biosphere reserve concept.

Successful management of the Marine Park depends largely on users and visitors respecting zoning and other regulations. The Authority's major concern is to heighten people's awareness of the environment and the problems that can occur. The result, hopefully, is an increasing sense of personal commitment and responsibility, not only to the preservation of the Reef but to all of Australia's natural environment. The Authority recognises that attempting management by surveillance and enforcement must remain subsidiary to the education of the public. The Marine Park is enormous — it has no walls, roads or gates that can be shut. Relying on enforcement and surveillance alone would be prohibitively expensive and next to impossible.

Nevertheless, surveillance, by air or by vessel, provides a valuable management tool. Knowledge is gained about usage patterns, location of vessels, apparent infringements and major natural occurrences such as cay formation or aggregations of seabirds, turtles and dugong. All of this information is used to administer and manage the Reef effectively.

HISTORY AND CULTURE

Cultural heritage, too, is an important aspect of the Reef's significance. Its northern sector in particular, is an integral part of the history and culture of the Aborigines of the coastal areas of north-east Australia. For over 40 000 years, and up to this day, the Reef has been used by the traditional inhabitants, mainly for the fishing and hunting of turtles and dugong. When Europeans arrived Aborigines were using 20-metre double outrigger canoes to travel to the outer islands. Further south the canoes were smaller but could still be used to travel such distances. Middens and archaeological sites of Aboriginal and Torres Strait origin are found in this area, and more exploration by divers may help to make early Aboriginal history on the north-eastern coast less obscure.

From a European point of view, the Reef's northern sector is the site of 30 historic shipwrecks, island lighthouses, and ruins of cultural and historic interest. It is also one of the main areas with which Captain Cook is associated. Having sailed for over 1000 kilometres along the coast to Queensland, between the outer reefs and the mainland, Cook realised that escape from this complex maze of individual reefs was imperative. The *Endeavour* was saved from being blown into a reef only by desperate measures — cannons were jettisoned and the crew, using the rowboat, towed the ship back into deep water. Edging their way carefully up the coast they passed two islands (Hope Islands), failed to find a harbour in the shallow Weary Bay (named in deference to the tired rowers) and eventually found the mouth of the Endeavour River — the site of Cooktown — where they were able to repair their beleaguered ship. From here, Cook sailed eastward to the Coral Sea. Reaching Lizard Island he climbed a hill to look for a break in the reef and, choosing a path later known as Cook's Passage, reached the open sea in safety.

White settlement brought conflict along the Queensland coast, with Aborigines retaliating in the face of white violence. A gradual change in the uses of the area ensued. Aborigines became part of the newly-established maritime industries, gathering shells and bêche-de-mer, the oriental delicacy made from dried and smoked sea cucumbers, and were also seconded into local shipping activity. A large industry developed around diving for pearl oyster shells and Trochus and Turban shells used to make mother-of-pearl buttons.

RECREATION AND TOURISM

Changes occurred again in the 1950s when the Reef became increasingly used for fishing and recreation, still its major activities. The 1960s saw a major development in commercial fishing and by 1965 there were 250 vessels trawling the Reef. In 1983 the figure stood at 1400. Surprisingly, perhaps, recreational fishing accounts for as much as 70 per cent of fin fish caught on the Great Barrier Reef.

Tourism has been growing steadily since the 1950s, and is now the Reef's major industry. Advances in technology in the 1980s have meant much more rapid escalation. Fast catamarans can now transport visitors to the reefs and islands in a fraction of the time it had previously taken. Semi-submersibles make the spectacular sights and colours of the Reef accessible to all. Despite all the changes, over the last two centuries in particular, little impact has been made on the Reef itself. Damage and disturbance to this remarkable natural wonder has been limited to a few specific cases.

The measures introduced by the Great Barrier Reef Marine Park Authority are designed to prevent any further damage occurring. Conservation is the first priority, and the resources available for use are, therefore, those that are living and renewable. These are mainly food — fish and crustaceans such as prawns — and more exotic products such as trochus shell and bêche-de-mer. Industries have grown up around these and other resources. In the early 1980s the trochus shell industry once more began to flourish as the collection of hard coral and shells became an integral part of the tourist industry.

Another significant industry and one likely to see future growth is the aquarium industry. Today licenced collectors remove fish and selected invertebrates from the Reef. They are valuable both locally and for export but ultimately they must move from a hunting to a cultivation base.

Much is still to be done, to ensure that the resources of the Reef are conserved whilst still being used and appreciated. Farming techniques have been introduced to prevent supplies from dwindling. Pioneers in this field were the pearl oyster growers, the first to recognise the need for stock replenishment. Now increasing attention is being given to mariculture by the fishing industry as both recreational and commercial demand for fish and prawns escalate.

Protection of rare and endangered species has also become a priority. The reef contains the world's only large herds of dugong, and it is now recognised that dugong have been killed easily in the past when ensnared in fishermen's nets. Raine Island is the site of the world's largest mass breeding ground for turtles, and careless use of this and other breeding grounds has been prevented. Throughout the Reef are hundreds of breeding sites for seabirds, damaged in the past by the effects of human habitation and interference, whether deliberate or accidental. Rats, for example, which probably swam ashore from disease-ridden ships of the past centuries, have been responsible for the destruction of nestlings and eggs. Feral goats have also been responsible for severe habitat degradation on many of the islands.

Before the establishment of the Marine Park Authority much less was known about the extraordinary ecosystem of the Great Barrier Reef. Continued research, undertaken by scientists of many diverse disciplines, has provided invaluable information on the nature of the Reef. It has also meant a greater understanding of the best and most effective means of conservation. That includes not only protecting the Reef, but also its surrounding areas and the wildlife that is an integral part of its existence, its beauty and its fascination.

A WORLD HERITAGE SITE

In the second century B.C. the writer Antipater of Sidon drew up a list of the seven wonders of the world. The Pyramids of Egypt, the oldest of the seven, is the only wonder still substantially in existence. Since then the seven wonders of the natural world have been designated — Mount Everest, Victoria Falls, the Grand Canyon, Northern Lights, Paricutin in Mexico, Rio de Janeiro harbour and the Great Barrier Reef. In 1981 the Reef was inscribed on the World Heritage list, affirming its significance to the world community.

The Reef meets the criteria set out in Article 2 of the World Heritage Convention on the basis that:

- It is an outstanding representation of a major stage of the earth's evolutionary history.

- It is an outstanding example of significant ongoing geological processes, biological evolution and man's interaction with his natural environment.
- It contains unique, rare and superlative natural phenomena, formations and features and areas of exceptional natural beauty.
- It provides habitats where populations of rare and endangered species of plants and animals still survive.

The Reef also meets all the required conditions for integrity. It contains all or nearly all the key interrelated and interdependent elements necessary for the continuation of its being and its continued development, and for the preservation of the species which inhabit it.

Beautiful *Tubastrea* corals grow in the shade, in caves and under ledges. Unlike most corals they lack symbiotic algae, the colours are their own.

EVOLUTION

DAVID HOPLEY

CORAL reefs are the marine equivalent of tropical rainforests. Both are complex tropical ecosystems with enormous biological diversity and productivity. Their complexity is expressed in an extreme interdependence of plants and animals. Both ecosystems are characterised by high temperatures and high energy levels. The ecosystems themselves can modify their environments, producing a whole array of microsystems each with its own community. For example, the microclimate of the floor of a tropical rainforest, with its low light levels, lack of air movement and constant humidity, is quite different from the microclimate of the canopy. Similarly, the lagoon or back reef zone of a coral reef contrasts strongly with the high energy windward margins upon which the waves of the open ocean break.

Most importantly, however, both systems are very efficient at nutrient cycling. Surprisingly, in areas of such biological abundance, mineral foods required to sustain life are relatively scarce. Rainforest soils are quickly depleted of these mineral nutrients which are normally stored within the plants themselves and subsequently return to the soils when the plants die. Similarly, tropical ocean waters are very low in mineral nutrients. Coral reefs are attuned to this situation and the lower plants in particular play important parts in fixing and conserving nutrients. Finally, the variety of forms displayed by both rainforests and coral reefs has developed over a very long time.

Part of the Pompey Complex. Although clearly visible from the air most of this reef is in fact under water.

THE ORIGIN OF AUSTRALIAN REEFS

Corals are one of the oldest forms of animal life, dating back at least 500 million years. One hundred million years ago reefs flourished in Australia, building up enormous systems equivalent to that of the Great Barrier Reef. The Limestone Ranges in the Canning Basin of Western Australia were formed from a barrier reef at least as impressive as the present Queensland reef system. However, the modern reef-building corals evolved about 230 million years ago at which time Australia was not in a position to provide an environment suitable for reef growth.

The earth's surface is dynamic. Erosion caused by rain, wind, ice and waves is not the only agent of change. Great slabs of the earth's crust, known as plates, move about on the earth's surface and new crust is constantly being created along the great volcanic ridges in the centres of the oceans. It was the division of neighbouring plates which resulted in California's San Andreas fault. Collision, on the other hand, will form great mountain chains such as the Alps and Himalayas.

The Great Barrier Reef is the largest living structure in the world and is clearly visible from outer space.

Thus, at the time when the modern reef-building corals first evolved, the continent that is now Australia was located close to the south pole and formed part of a super-continent called Gondwanaland, made up of the present southern hemisphere land masses of Antarctica, South America, Africa, India and Australia. The waters were far too cold for coral reefs to grow. Only after Gondwanaland started to break up and the sections of the plate on which Australia was located commenced to drift northwards, did the waters around Australia start to warm. This was about 75 million years ago.

By 12 million years ago, the northern tip of what is now the Great Barrier Reef migrated into the warm intertropical waters suitable for coral growth and reefs started to develop. New Guinea, located on the northern section of the plate which Australia occupies, was coming into contact with the larger plate of the Pacific Ocean and acquired reefs earlier. The collision of the plates crumpled the crust, forming the Owen Stanley Ranges and raising the early reefs thousands of metres above sea level. In contrast, the Great Barrier Reef began to form on an evolving and subsiding continental shelf. The northern part of this shelf entered the tropics first, and it is here that the foundations of the Great Barrier Reef are oldest. They gradually become younger towards the south which entered the tropics last. Much of the central and southern Great Barrier Reef may be no more than two million years old. The largest reef system of the earth is also one of the youngest.

CORAL REEFS AND SEA LEVEL CHANGE

This period of reef formation coincided with rapid changes of sea level resulting from the formation of large ice sheets, first in Antarctica, then in Greenland and finally over the continental land masses of north-west Europe and north America. Ice up to 4 000 metres thick extracted large amounts of water from the oceans and at the height of each glacial episode sea levels subsided by as much as 150 metres, exposing the entire continental shelf and leaving the ancestors of our modern reefs high and dry. Every 120 000 years or so, however, a proportion of the ice melted and sea level rose to about its present position, remaining there each time for about 10 000 years. Once more the continental shelves and their reefs were underwater

An underwater view of a typical section of the reef looking towards the surface.

The brilliant white sand of Frigate Cay stands out in contrast to the submerged Swain Reefs.

and new corals and other limestone-producing plants and animals grew as living reefs. During the intervening low sea level periods, the biota of coral reefs were forced to migrate to the steeply sloping continental slopes and to the submerged plateaux of ocean basins, such as the Queensland Plateau in the northern Coral Sea.

Reef growth has therefore been restricted to relatively short periods of high sea level. Calcium carbonate in the form of limestone was laid down by a great variety of plants and animals. During the longer periods of low sea level and exposure, the reef was subjected to wind and weather. Parts were eroded and, as the reef is a limestone structure, chemical etching was particularly effective in producing land-forms typical of all limestone regions. These are characterised by little surface drainage, but have enclosed depressions in which solution forms sink holes and cave systems. These features formed on the exposed reef and when sea level rose again, they formed the foundation for the shape of the new reef. Much of the intricate relief of modern reefs, such as lagoons, reef rims and channels, is thought to derive from these landforms.

Typically, the thickness of reef added during a high sea level episode is about 10 to 15 metres. As recently as 18 000 years ago, sea level was 150 metres below its present position, but rose so rapidly that by 9 000 years ago, it was high enough to have covered much of the continental shelf, drowning the older reef foundations and initiating modern reef growth. Sea level has been relatively stable over the last 6 000 years, and although many of the reefs still mimic the shape of their eroded foundations, others have had time to grow up to sea level and develop extensive reef flats.

THE REEF BUILDERS

CORAL POLYPS AND CORAL COLONIES

The coral polyps are the organisms producing the essential building bricks of large and complex reefs. They are the simplest organisms to have discrete nervous, muscular and reproductive systems and are related to jellyfish and anemones. Their soft tissue comprises tentacles with stinging cells called nematocysts, a centrally placed mouth and a body cavity with walls composed of two cell layers. This inner cell layer is the site of one of the most remarkable symbiotic relationships in nature, playing host to enormous numbers of unicellular algae, approximately 0.01 millimetres in diameter. These are termed the *zooxanthellae* and have great importance for corals and coral reefs.

The polyp lays down a skeleton or *corallite*, a cup-like form with internal dividing plates called *septa*, the arrangement of which forms the basis of species classification. The skeleton is made up of limestone, a type of calcium carbonate known as aragonite. Some corals, such as the mushroom corals, live singly as individuals, but most are colonial with individual polyps gradually growing outwards and dividing into two. Individual species, however, may take on various colonial lifeforms and varying colours. Life form is largely dependent on position on the reef, with availability of light and wave energy the most important controls. For example, where light level is low, corals form large plates making the best use of the light available but they can only do this below the level of vigorous wave action. By contrast, in the surface zone, corals are short, stubby and strong so that they can resist the breaking of the waves, and at the highest part of the reef the corals may give way to crustose coralline algae (plants which grow as hard calcium carbonate skins over the surface of the reef). Colour in corals is largely controlled by the pigmentation of the zooxanthellae concentrated in the tissue. The colour of corals is therefore confined to the living tissue and not to the underlying skeleton which is invariably white limestone.

A typical section of reef flat just north of Lark Pass, showing crustose coralline algal surface with small branching corals.

22

The brilliance of the soft coral has been reflected in these two fish which make it their home.

The minute plants, the zooxanthellae, are important to the coral in a number of ways. In return for the space to live and the consumption of polyp waste products such as phosphates and nitrates used as nutrients, the zooxanthellae supply the coral with as much as 98 per cent of its total food requirements. They also take a direct part in the laying down of the coral skeleton through processes of photosynthesis which in turn control the amount of calcium carbonate held in the solutions of the coral's body tissue. Coral growth in daylight is two to three times more rapid than in darkness. Growth rates for coral colonies are fastest in shallow, well-lit waters and can be up to 2 centimetres a year for the massive corals, while branching colonies may extend by as much as 10 centimetres a year.

Not all corals lay down a hard skeleton. Soft corals, which are more common on inshore reefs, can take over areas of hard coral substrate damaged by cyclones or crown-of-thorns starfish. Some contain spicules of calcium carbonate in their rubbery tissue and these contribute to the reef sediments after death.

These algal ridges at Cockermouth Island are typical examples of how plants can dominate part of the reef top.

THE IMPORTANCE OF PLANTS

Plants, particularly algae, may not be the most obvious members of the coral reef ecosystem, but they are a vital component. Although nutrient conservation is possibly less critical on the Great Barrier Reef than in open ocean waters because minerals such as nitrate, phosphate and iron can be introduced from mainland run-off or by upwelling of rich deep ocean water on the shelf edge, nonetheless the foodlinks and trophic structure of the reef are directed towards nutrient cycling. Photosynthesis provides the bulk of the organic carbon required to sustain the organisms of the reef. Towards the poleward limits of reef growth or in situations where inorganic nutrients may be higher than normal, plants, particularly macroalgae such as *Sargassum*, may outgrow the corals. However, on most reefs the algae, though providing the basis in the food chain, are kept in check by herbivorous fish, another example of interdependence in the ecosystem.

The importance of plants cannot be overstressed. It has already been seen that the minute zooxanthellae form much of the food for corals and aid in the formation of their skeletons. Algae are the primary source of energy for all other reef organisms. Like all plants they capture light energy and use this to convert carbon dioxide into organic carbon by photosynthesis. This organic carbon enters the food chain by herbivorous animals or is consumed in the water column by bacteria which in turn may be consumed by a wide range of filter feeders.

Primary production by algae also involves the incorporation of inorganic nitrogen from dissolved nitrates and ammonium. Microscopic blue-green algae are vital nitrogen fixers in a system which is poor in nitrogen and this can account for 20 to 40 per cent of the overall need of reefs. The algae also act as nutrient sinks or recyclers. Periodic upwellings of nutrient rich deep water may result in short term algal blooms that will incorporate nutrients in the reef sediments when they die.

Plants also help to build up the reef structure. The crustose coralline forms are found on the high energy reef rims, and other plants, such as *Halimeda*, have plate-like structures made up of calcium carbonate that, after the death of the plant, can form up to 80 per cent of reef sediments. These sediments, to which may be added the skeletal remains of many animals and other plants, help to fill in the voids of the reef structure and contribute to the formation of coral cays.

Finally, plants also contribute to the breakdown of reef limestone. Some boring algae can penetrate the dead skeletons of corals, breaking them up into sediments as part of the process of bioerosion.

Plants, particularly algae, are so important to coral reefs that they help to determine the distribution of corals. As they need to photosynthesise, availability of light is a very critical ecological control.

This small bead-like green algae, *Caulerpa*, helps to bind together the reef top sediments produced by bioerosion.

The pink crusting coralline algae help to bind together the Reef structure.

PLANT DOMINATION

When the sea level first rose and flooded the continental shelf, the corals did not migrate back onto their older foundations immediately. This delay was due to the need for migration of suitable coral stock from distant refuges — and the need for suitable ocean currents. Initially, after inundation of the older reef foundations, high turbidity may also have been a detrimental factor as soils were partially removed from the older reef foundations and a mainland coastline with sediment-laden rivers migrated back across the shelves of the continent to what was to become the modern reef tract.

Much recent work on the Great Barrier Reef has suggested that during this early period of flooding, much of the outer reef area was dominated by vegetation composed almost entirely of the green calcareous alga *Halimeda*. For a short period between about 12 000 and 8 000 years ago, conditions may have been far more suitable for plant growth on the Great Barrier Reef than they were for the corals, and great banks consisting of the remains of these calcareous plants formed in what are presently water depths of between 30 and 50 metres. These banks have been identified on the outer shelf of the Great Barrier Reef along almost its entire length and are typically 15 to 20 metres high. They are still covered by plants, including *Halimeda*, but do not appear to be growing as rapidly as they did 8 000 years ago.

This outer (seaward) area of Reef which is affected by wave energy is typically dominated by large concentrations of algae.

A period of rapid growth probably resulted from a number of factors which included the high nutrient levels in the nearshore waters of the time. As sea level was still low, the mainland coastline and its sediment-laden streams were much closer to the outer edge of the shelf. In addition, oceanic circulation probably resulted in rich oceanic water upwelling onto the edge of the shelf at that time. Nutrients were also being released by the re-working of the soils of the previously exposed coastal plains. All these factors favoured plant growth and the *Halimeda* banks, found, for example, behind the northern ribbon reefs, are an important inheritance dating from this period of early shelf flooding.

CORAL ECOLOGY AND REEF PRODUCTION

Reef building corals and their symbiotic algae require very specific conditions to flourish. On a worldwide scale, temperature is the most important factor, as reefs are mainly limited to tropical waters. Below about 18°C, coral growth is so slow that bioerosion may be faster than the formation of reef framework and other competitors for shallow water substrates such as kelp or *Sargassum*, may take over. Coral reproduction also is affected at lower temperatures. Since ocean currents vary in temperature they have a global influence on the establishment of coral reefs. Noticeably the western sides of oceans, which receive water from other warm equatorial regions, have a preponderance of coral reefs. In contrast the dominant currents on the eastern sides of oceans are usually from reef-less (and colder) higher latitudes.

More locally, salinity may become important since corals require salinities close to those of the open ocean (about 35 parts per thousand). Reefs cannot develop

The enormous run-off of sediment from the Murray River in North Queensland after cyclone Winifred.

in waters which receive freshwater run-off, nor can they thrive in enclosed basins or lagoons where salinity may be too high, often in combination with elevated temperatures. The sediments carried by rivers may also be lethal to corals and coral reefs. Although they may be able to withstand small amounts of sediment because polyps can remove some from their surfaces by movement of their tentacles, they cannot withstand heavy sedimentation and burial. Sediment concentrations in the water column also cut down the amount of light which is so important to the algae. In clear open ocean water, corals can be found to depths greater than 100 metres. In highly turbid inshore waters, there may be insufficient light in depths as little as 10 metres.

These polyps are just beginning to release their gametes as part of the vast synchronised coral spawning.

However, in environments with suitable temperatures and salinities together with low turbidity, corals will flourish and successfully reproduce. Asexual reproduction by polyp division is the way in which a colony expands, but sexual reproduction producing planula larvae is the means of long distance dispersal and the way in which corals can cross genetically with each other. The males of some corals release sperm that swim to females for internal fertilisation. This usually happens when the same species are in close proximity. For many corals, however, fertilisation is external, with both males and females releasing their gametes (sperm and eggs) into the water. The chance of genetic mixing is thus increased. As currents can quickly disperse eggs and sperm, different colonies of the same species synchronise their spawning, with perhaps half of all corals on the Great Barrier Reef doing this over a few nights.

This spectacular spawning event commences just after sunset about five days after the full moon, when currents are at their weakest. It occurs during early summer or late spring, the time of year when water temperature is rising. This mass spawning has only recently been observed and documented, but sufficient is now known that it can be forecast quite accurately for different parts of the reef.

Mass spawning produces planula larvae, which are up to 1.6 millimetres long, and can swim actively. Many planulae appear to settle within a few hours, often on the same reef. Others may drift as plankton for days or weeks before settling on suitable substrate hundreds of kilometres away from their parent colony. Only a very small fraction of the millions of eggs which are produced will be fertilised and will be successfully recruited to a reef, a pattern of reproduction and recruitment which is common to many reef organisms, including the crown-of-thorns starfish.

DIVERSITY OF CORAL SPECIES

The Great Barrier Reef lies on the southern side of the tropical zone in which the greatest diversity of coral species occurs. Over 60 genera and 330 species of coral are found on the Reef. Even at its southern limit there are more than 230 species present. Each species has its own niche in the reef system as it competes with others for space, light and food, but with so many species present the result is a microcosm of complex but distinctive communities. In fact so complex have the coral assemblages become that sophisticated statistical techniques are needed to differentiate between them.

On individual reefs, the major determinants of community type are light and wave energy. Light varies with depth on the reef slope, and wave energy varies from reef front to leeward edge or lagoon resulting in a series of narrow zones parallel

Just below the reef crest where wave action is strong corals grow with short, thick branches.

to the reef front. Whilst latitudinal variation between reefs may be small, great contrasts occur across the continental shelf, controlled by fresh water and the build-up of silt close to land and high wave energy towards the ocean.

The greatest diversity of both species and community types is found on reefs near the middle of the continental shelf. Oceanic reefs and those near shore are much less diverse. Nutrition is also important. Coral reefs near the mainland obtain much of their nutrition from the surrounding environment. Reefs on the outermost shelf generate nearly all of their own nutrition. Mid-shelf locations have the highest diversity because they contain corals of both types.

Community structure, however, is dynamic: composition and diversity are not only a function of environmental preferences. The magnitude and frequency of major disturbances (such as storms) increase the diversity of the ensuing recolonisation. Damage caused by tropical cyclones and by crown-of-thorns starfish is comparable to the effect of forest fires: destruction leads to the introduction of many fast growing species, a rapidly changing secondary succession and some 'fire resistant' colonies such as large *Porites* heads. These can grow up to 5 metres in diameter and are often hundreds of years old.

Corals dominate the appearance of particular habitats and thereby form the basis for community description. On outer slopes, where the water is clear, extensive coral growth may occur at depths of over 100 metres. For example, on recent submersible dives off Myrmidon Reef on the outer shelf off Townsville, scattered corals were found to depths of 110 metres. The corals are mainly thin, brittle, encrusting plates making the most of the low light availability. At 70 metres coral cover is total with monospecific stands of plate and foliaceous corals determined by light availability. Above 50 metres, coral cover becomes dense and moderately diverse, composed according to water clarity, currents and steepness of the reef slope. From 20 metres upwards light is not a limiting factor and species diversity is at a maximum with very mixed communities and varied growth forms. Reef fronts are exposed to wave action and the degree of exposure generally determines the species composition, though all are short and stocky. Coralline algae may dominate the outer reef flats while inner reef flats may have good coral cover, consisting mostly of branching *Acropora* species, and hardy coral heads. Back reef margins have very active coral growth, usually dominated by massive *Porites* and other head corals. These reef slopes are very irregular but have a lush and varied coral growth; many of the rarer coral genera can be found here together with soft corals, sea whips and sea fans.

THE REEF METABOLISM

The link between the biological and geological environment is the manufacture by plants and animals of calcium carbonate that creates the coral reef framework and sediments. The reef, however, is the net product of a wide range of processes as not all biological activity is directed towards construction. There is a large number of bioeroders scraping, boring and etching into the limestone and, in stressful conditions such as those produced by pollution, the net loss from the reef system may be greater than the gain from calcification. Many bioeroders, such as worms, some molluscs and sponges, use acid secretions to bore into the coral substrate. Some are very small. Microborers include blue-green algae, bacteria and fungii: they are so effective at breaking down corals into rubble and silt that they can reduce a coral head in a matter of a few years. Indicative of the rates at which calcium carbonate can be broken down are those recorded for boring sponges. These can remove or break down up to seven kilograms of calcium carbonate in every square metre of the reef each year.

Rich coral growth of the upper slope. Where wave action is not too strong corals branch to create a varied landscape.

Many organisms feed on the algae growing on the reef substrate and, as they graze, their rasping, scraping or biting action also removes a fine layer of hard substrate. Grazers include a wide variety of fish, especially parrot fish, as well as sea urchins and a range of molluscs including snails, limpets and chitons. Again as an example, a single chiton can consume up to 18 cubic centimetres of substrate each year. Holothurians, or sea cucumbers, pass up to 40kg of algal-covered sand through their gut each year and, as the gut is partially acid, the sand may be subjected to some solution.

Bioeroders, such as worms, sponges, sea cucumbers and sea urchins effectively break down corals into rubble and silt.

The overall result is that different parts of the reef will be producing and reducing limestone at different rates. The total process is called community or reef metabolism and can be measured in terms of organic productivity. Because the reef ecosystem supports more animal and plant species than any other system, productivity is prodigious and has been estimated at over 80 tonnes for each hectare of reef each year, or twelve times the existing biomass. Gross production of calcium carbonate may be as high as 35kg for each square metre a year, but much of this is lost through bioerosion and other processes, and the maximum net rate which can be sustained by an area with 100% coral cover, is about 10kg for each metre of reef each year. However, the rates vary greatly in different zones of the reef and over sand and rubble areas may be as little as one twentieth of this figure.

Reef metabolic performance can be measured almost instantaneously and enough is now known about natural environmental and seasonal fluctuations that it is possible to say that similar environments with apparently different reef communities are likely to have very similar growth rates. Variations produced by stress, such as increased freshwater run-off or outflow of sewage over reefs may be picked up by measuring the reef metabolism even before any obvious changes have taken place in the existing communities.

32

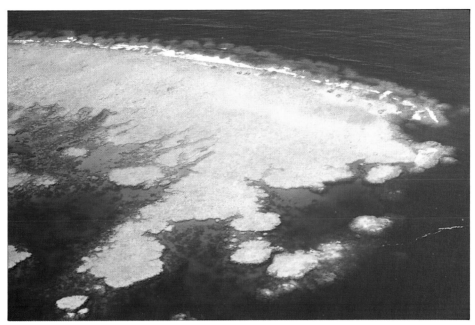

Moss Reef is a good example of a fringing reef with its seaward section taking the brunt of wave action and the exposed reef flats behind.

THE GREAT BARRIER REEF MOSAIC

The term 'Great Barrier Reef' is a misnomer for it is made up of over 2 900 individual reefs, about 750 of which are fringing reefs attached to the mainland or the numerous islands of the Queensland coastline. Almost 2 150 are outer reefs. It forms a true near-continuous barrier only in its most northern third. The outer perimeter of the Reef is about 2 300 kilometres long, the largest reef system the earth has ever seen and quite easily visible from space. Its southernmost tip is just south of Gladstone at Lady Elliot Island (24°07' S) and it extends northwards into the Gulf of Papua to about 9°15' S. The Great Barrier Reef Marine Park ends at 10°41' S opposite the tip of Cape York and thus does not include the numerous reefs of Torres Strait. Reefs vary in size from small isolated pinnacles to massive structures over 25 kilometres in length and 125 square kilometres in area. In some parts of the region they are closely spaced but elsewhere there may be several kilometres of open water between reefs. The total reef area is just over 20 000 square kilometres which represents about 9 per cent of the total area of the continental shelf of the Marine Park.

In the north, to just south of Cooktown (see map), the outer barrier is formed by ribbon reefs. These are long (up to 25 kilometres) reefs about 500 metres wide and with narrow restricted passages between them. Behind this barrier is an area of apparently open water, but containing many of the *Halimeda* banks described earlier. Further shorewards are numerous closely spaced reefs with large areas of reef flat exposed at low tide, many with small sand banks and vegetated coral islands (cays). The innermost reefs, often no more than 8 kilometres from the mainland,

Kangaroo Complex showing narrow tidal channel between large reefs and intricate closed lagoons.

sometimes have not only vegetated coral cays but also large areas of mangrove on the intertidal reef flat and are referred to as 'low wooded islands'. Even the outer reefs of this northern region may be only 30 kilometres from the mainland as the continental shelf is quite narrow here. High islands, made up of the continental rocks of the mainland, are infrequent, although those that do occur have extensive fringing reefs. Much of the mainland coastline, particularly where it is steep and rocky or close to a headland, also has narrow fringes of reef.

From Cairns southwards, the Reef changes. Opposite the Whitsunday Islands, the continental shelf gradually widens to about 125 kilometres and even the inner-most reefs may be 40 to 50 kilometres from shore. There is no outer barrier of ribbon reefs and although the main reef tract contains large and numerous reefs these are often in the form of crescentic outer rims and large sheltered backreef lagoons with coral patches. Fringing reefs are absent from the mainland but there are great numbers of continental islands, most of which do have fringing reefs. Coral cays with vegetation are completely lacking from this part of the Great Barrier Reef.

South of the Whitsunday Islands, there are further changes. There are still many continental islands, but the fringing reefs become smaller and more patchy. The outer barrier here is at least 90 kilometres from the mainland and the outermost reefs may be as much as 290 kilometres from land. It is unfortunate that they are so remote for they include some of the most closely spaced reefs of the entire Great Barrier Reef. The northern part of this section, known as the Pompey Complex, has narrow tidal channels between very large reefs with intricate closed lagoons. The southern part, the Swain Reefs, has much smaller but even more closely spaced reefs (599 reefs occur between latitude 21° and 22° S), many with small coral cays.

34

The narrow ribbon reefs of the far north section form the traditional reef pattern with few breaks for navigation.

This blue hole is not a crater from a meteorite but just a natural formation of coral in the Pompey complex.

The southern tip of the Swain Reefs is 200 kilometres from the mainland and separated from it by the Capricorn Channel. To the south the continental shelf region narrows and the southernmost reefs, the Bunker and Capricorn Groups, are little more than 50 kilometres from the mainland. These are particularly attractive reefs, many with large vegetated sand cays and distinctive sheltered lagoons.

The narrow tidal channels of the Pompey Complex are fast flowing between calm lagoons.

ISLANDS OF THE GREAT BARRIER REEF

There are two types of island found within the Great Barrier Reef: the high or continental islands, and the coral cays. Continental islands are made up of exactly the same rocks as the adjacent mainland and are partially drowned extensions of the mainland hills. There are over 2 000 continental islands in the Great Barrier Reef Marine Park area, and of these at least 750 have fringing reefs attached to them. Although the fringing reefs are subjected to greater stress from freshwater run-off and siltation than the outer reefs, they are nonetheless rich and diverse in coral species. After heavy run-off, freshwater may float as a lens on the surface of the sea and because of this, the reef flats of the fringing reefs may be dominated by algae. However, the slopes can be particularly rich. As water clarity is less than on the outer reefs, the whole zonation on the reef slope may be compressed into no more than 10 or 15 metres of water depth. This feature is even more pronounced on the mainland fringing reefs which are only found on the Queensland coastline north of Cairns. For example, the Cape Tribulation reefs contain 141 species, but the whole reef zonation is compacted into less than 8 metres depth of water.

Vegetation has grown over the sand dunes on Hinchinbrook Island, one of the larger continental islands.

Because the fringing reefs are easily accessible from the mainland, and the continental islands to which they are attached are frequently quite large, all but three of the Great Barrier Reef island resorts are located on high islands.

Islands composed entirely of debris produced by the reef itself are termed cays. Considerable quantities of sand and rubble are produced by coral reefs through the action of storms on the reef margins and the breakdown of corals through bioerosion. Where wave patterns and currents are suitable, this material may be swept into particular locations on the reef. Coarser rubble is sometimes concentrated on the windward side to form a shingle cay whilst sand is swept further back on the reef to form a sand cay.

Unlike the coral cays which are formed entirely of sand and coral rubble, some continental islands, such as Orpheus Island seen here, have boulder beaches.

Initially, the concentration of sediment may be highly mobile and the emerging cay will be washed over by every high tide. However, as high tides, storms and winds help build up a cay, the birds are attracted to it and often bring in the seeds of plants either in their digestive tracts or adhering to their plumage. Many foreshore plants also have seeds which float and such seeds may reach the new coral island. Initially the vegetation consists of low creepers, but as the island develops in size and becomes higher and more stable, shrubs start to grow and finally even large trees may become established. As the island continues to expand, particularly in areas of high rainfall, a brackish water lens develops beneath it and this allows the higher vegetation to flourish. Stability is also brought about by the waters percolating through the beach and cementing the outer part of the island sediments into what is termed beach rock. These concrete-like bastions further stabilise the cay.

Barnett Island is a perfect example of an unvegetated coral cay.

Bushy Island, a typical coral cay, where the vegetation has developed over the years.

Birds aid in ways other than providing seeds. As they nest and roost on the island, their droppings leach into the raw sands and help to enrich them for plant growth. These droppings, or guano, may accumulate sufficiently over thousands of years to produce concretionary layers which also help to stabilise the coral cay. However, such guano deposits were also very attractive as fertilisers and, particularly during the 1890s, a number of coral cays of the Great Barrier Reef were mined for their guano deposits.

There are over 300 cays within the Great Barrier Reef Marine Park area. Of these, about 90 are vegetated, though many have not progressed beyond the stage of low colonising creepers. North of Cairns are some 44 special types of islands which are referred to as low wooded islands. The southernmost and most frequently visited are the Low Isles off Port Douglas. These islands typically occur on reefs close to the mainland and consist of extensive rubble banks made up of coral shingle, particularly around their windward margins, in the lee of which can grow extensive areas of mangroves. Many low wooded islands also have small vegetated sand cays towards their leeward side. As they lie along the inner shipping channel, these islands are often the location of navigational beacons.

Only three coral islands have tourist resorts established upon them: Green Island, Heron Island and Lady Elliot Island. Difficulties of access, frequent erosion of cays during storms, lack of water and the general fragility of coral cay environments mean that it is highly unlikely that further resorts will be established on the cays although they will remain major tourist attractions for day visits.

MICROATOLLS

AN EXAMPLE OF CORAL INTERACTION

Corals cannot withstand long periods above water and their upper limit of growth is approximately that of Low Water Spring Tide. On the edge of the reef, particularly to windward, some variation in the level of growth may occur as different species have different tolerances to exposure and some in more exposed conditions may be kept moist at the lowest tides by waves breaking over them. However, as a particular

Tilted microatolls on Orpheus Island resemble large bowling balls.

species reaches its uppermost limit, it will stop growing upwàrds. Branching corals become stunted and will grow upwards only after a storm has removed the uppermost growth tips. Massive corals respond differently, and as they reach their limit, the top surface of the corals will first become bleached (a process which involves the expulsion of the zooxanthellae) and then finally, during a period of particularly warm weather coinciding with low tides, the uppermost surface will die. The sides of the corals, however, will continue to grow outwards, producing what is termed a microatoll form. This consists of a coral colony with a living and growing rim and a dead top. In open water, the dead top is usually sloping and careful observation will reveal that the majority slope in one direction. Invariably, the highest living rim is on the southern side and the sloping top faces to the north. So consistent is this pattern that their orientation could almost be used as a compass. Although the southern

Reef crest corals as seen at Gable Reef, have a limited growth once they are exposed to the air.

side of the colonies may grow slightly higher due to the prevailing wave direction, this is not the main reason for the shape. The sloping microatoll form is a response to the direction of the sun during the winter when excessively low daytime tides occur. The southern side of the colony is shaded and therefore does not desiccate as quickly as the northern edge. It therefore grows to a level approximately 10 centimetres higher than the opposite side.

Open water microatolls generally display the irregularities just described. However, very symmetrical forms are found in the pools which become stranded at low tide on the reef top. As the levels of such pools are exactly the same on every high tide, since they are frequently moated behind shingle embankments which have been thrown up during cyclones, the coral colony will grow to this same level and produce a very flat top and surrounding living edge. This is the classic microatoll. They are particularly fascinating features of reef tops as they may indicate changes which have

The effect of the heavy rainfall on microatolls when they are exposed at low tide causes them to die back and results in a clearly defined ring.

A microatoll tilted by a tropical cyclone continues to grow outwards at the new adjusted water level.

taken place. For example, a major storm may breach the shingle dam causing a lowering of the water level and the microatoll will subsequently grow at a level lower than its former growth surface, forming a top hat type of shape. Even events such as heavy rainfall on a low tide may be recorded by microatolls as fresh water will cause some to die back and subsequently result in a clearly defined ring in the microatoll's top.

A RECORD OF ENVIRONMENTAL HISTORY

Clearly, microatolls can record particular meteorological events on a reef top. However, corals can contain even more subtle records of environmental changes. Typically, large coral heads such as *Porites* grow at a rate of about 1 centimetre per year. In the period leading up to spawning (late spring) much of the energy of the coral goes into reproduction and there is a slowing down of skeletal deposition.

During the rest of the year, the coral colony grows more rapidly. The result is that the 1 centimetre growth consists of two bands: a narrow high density band and a wider low density band which can be easily identified by x-ray photography in much the same way as growth rings on trees. A 5 metre diameter coral head may thus record up to 500 years of growth with each individual year being estimated back from the present living surface. Some very large heads have been shown to contain over a thousand years of continuous history. The actual size of the growth band may indicate how favourable or otherwise the ambient environment was in a particular year for coral growth.

Even more subtle variation can be picked up from geochemical analysis. Oxygen isotopes will provide information on the temperature of the water in which the coral was growing at any particular time whilst minute amounts of particular minerals, such as strontium, incorporated in the skeleton, can indicate how much nutrient, such as phosphate, was contained in that water. This phosphate may come directly from the land by natural erosion, by accelerated erosion following forest clearance, through the use of fertilisers for agriculture or through release of sewage into the marine environment. On the outer edge of the reef, phosphate may be incorporated through periodic upwelling produced, for example, by the cyclical El Nino event, and be recorded in the coral skeleton.The Little Ice Age which occurred in the seventeenth and eighteenth centuries involved a worldwide climatic change. This has been detected in the coral record, not only from oxygen isotopes, but also from the radioactive carbon derived from the atmosphere. Even the commencement of the nuclear age, with the explosion of atomic bombs in the 1940s and 1950s, can be detected in the coral skeletons.

Rainfall and run-off can be recorded by reefs which are within the area of influence of major rivers since the flow from such rivers during flood contains organic acids and these are incorporated in the skeleton. When subjected to ultra violet light, the concentration of these acids causes fluorescence of the corals, the degree of fluorescence corresponding to the amount of run-off in a particular year. A very good correlation has been found between the degree of fluorescence in corals in the Townsville region and the known run-off record for the Burdekin River. As the corals are older than the oldest of the measured records, the run-off period has been extrapolated back beyond the time of European settlement.

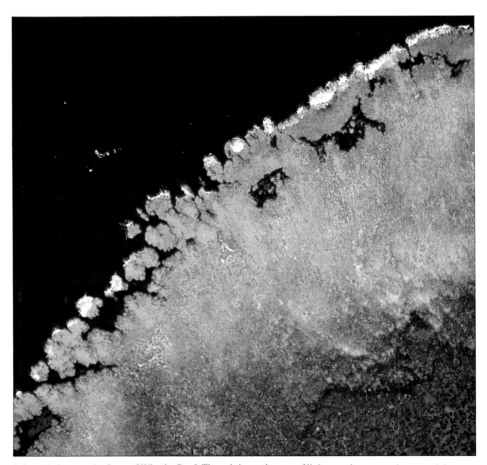

Infra-red photograph of part of Wheeler Reef. The red shows the area of living coral concentration around the margins of the Reef.

HISTORY AND EXPLORATION

R O N   C O L E M A N

THE first people to visit and inhabit the area which is now delimited by Australia's Great Barrier Reef were the forerunners of the modern Australian Aborigines. Human settlement of the continent by these hunter-gatherers from the South-East Asian region was widespread prior to 30 000 years ago. During the last Ice Age, which ended as recently as 6 000 years ago, the sea level was much lower than it is today. New Guinea, the Australian mainland, and the island of Tasmania were all one continent. Most of the continental shelf, including that part on which the Great Barrier Reef rests today, was dry land. As the Ice Age ended, the sea level slowly rose and gradually inundated the lower-lying areas of the giant island continent causing the coastal tribes to retreat to higher ground. Tasmania and New Guinea became separated from Australia by wide straits and the submerged shelf off the eastern coast of Queensland began to be populated by marine organisms, such as corals, and grow into an enormously complex reef system.

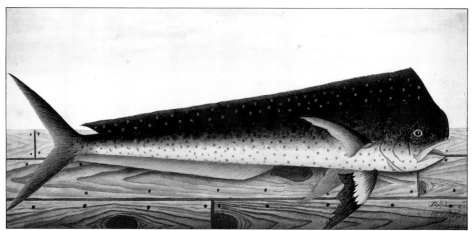

One of the earliest records of life on the Great Barrier Reef is this painting of a dolphin painted by G W Raper in 1794.

The natives of Australia did not develop traditions of sea-faring although they undoubtedly made some use of the Barrier Reef as a source of food from time to time.

Approximately 6 000 years ago, there was a second wave of migration into the coastal regions of New Guinea from South-East Asia. The newcomers brought with them later cultural developments. The most important of these, which stimulated territorial expansion, was the use of the sail and outrigger canoe. Ultimately, this innovation led to the discovery and population of the islands of at least the western Pacific as well as easy access to the eastern coast of Australia and the Great Barrier Reef. The Torres Strait, with its many islands and relatively protected water, became, once again, an avenue of intercourse between the two land masses. With time, a system of trade developed. The Aborigines of Cape York Peninsula traded ochre and weapons for finely made canoes from New Guinea.

Thus, it was not necessary for the early Australians to develop a strong boat-building tradition. Also, being a hunter-gatherer based culture, there was no compelling reason to venture very far from the Australian coast. As a result, the Aborigines, as opposed to other central Pacific cultures, did not develop open sea navigational skills. The possession of sturdy canoes did, however, lead to increased use of semi-protected waters such as those within the Barrier Reef. Turtle, dugong, shellfish and fish were more accessible. Mobility increased. Off-shore islands and new coastal regions could be reached easily.

To date, no positive proof of non-Austronesian visits to the Barrier Reef pre-dating Torres (1606) have been found. However, the penetration of Torres Strait from the west by Asiatics prior to that date is a very real possibility. Sixteenth century Portuguese and seventeenth century Dutch documents mention in passing Asian and Moorish traders visiting the south coast of New Guinea (which at that time was considered to extend to the bottom of the Gulf of Carpentaria), and that occasionally boats from the Aru Islands, south of the western tip of New Guinea, were blown hundreds of miles off-course toward Australia by the Northwest Monsoons.

A very old cave painting, found in 1985 by the author on Booby Island at the western entrance to the Strait, depicts a sailing vessel similar to a South-East Asian prau. It may eventually prove to be the earliest material evidence thus discovered relating to a non-Austronesian visit to the Strait and suggests possible penetration to the Barrier Reef on the eastern side.

The first European contact with the Great Barrier Reef system for which we have any documentary evidence was that of the Spaniard Luis Baez de Torres in 1606. Torres commanded one of the vessels on a voyage of exploration led by Pedro Fernandez de Quiros. At Espiritu Santo, in the New Hebrides, the ships were separated and Torres decided to proceed to Manila in accordance with sealed orders from his Viceroy. Sailing first to the south-west, in search of the suspected Terra Australis before turning north, he probably came to within 60 nautical miles of the Barrier Reef somewhere north-east of Rockhampton. Then, steering northward, he approached the outlying Louisiade Islands to the east of New Guinea. Not being able to steer more eastward due to the prevailing winds and seas, he turned west and found himself trapped beneath New Guinea. Following the coastline, Torres entered the Barrier Reef by passing around the northern end without knowing it. Finding his way barred by reefs in the strait which would eventually bear his name, he then turned south-west and was within the reef system. After some 40 days, Torres managed to thread his way through the many reefs and islands of the strait and continued on to Manila. The journals of his discoveries were kept secret by the Spaniards and details of the voyage were not rediscovered until 1765. This information was given to Joseph Banks for his voyage with Captain James Cook in 1768.

One other brief encounter with the Great Barrier Reef by a European pre-dates Cook's discovery by only two years. In 1768, the French explorer, the Chevalier de Bouganville was sailing west from Tahiti and turned away when he saw — 'an endless line of shoals and rocks on which the sea thundered with great violence. This last discovery was the voice of God and we were obedient to it.'

The discovery and charting of the eastern coastline of Australia had eluded explorers since the sixteenth century.

It took a man of Cook's daring and perseverance finally to succeed where the Spanish, Dutch and French had failed. Cook's first voyage, which began in 1768, had taken him through the South Pacific. In 1770, his six month survey of New Zealand completed and having spent more than a year and a half at sea, it was time to start thinking about returning to England. Barely six months of rations remained and *Endeavour's* sails and rigging were badly in need of repair. To return during the Atlantic gales of the winter months might prove to be too hazardous considering the ship's condition. Instead they would sail westward until they came to the eastern coast of New Holland (later to be named Australia), follow it northward and then proceed west again to the Dutch East Indies outpost of Batavia where they could revictual and repair the ship.

On the 19th of April, landfall was made. It was the extreme south-eastern corner of the continent which Cook named Point Hicks after the Lieutenant who first sighted it. The course was changed and the *Endeavour* sailed slowly northward along the coast.

A short time was spent at Botany Bay to replenish supplies of water and firewood before continuing the journey. On 6 June the ship arrived at Magnetic Island, so named because it seemed to affect the *Endeavour's* compass. Having followed the coastline, Cook was unaware of just how extensive the giant reef system which lay to seaward was. But, now it was becoming apparent that the further north they sailed, the closer the reef was to the mainland. On the night of 11 June, while gently sailing along under double-reefed topsails, *Endeavour* struck a submerged reef and stuck fast on the coral. The ship's boats and anchors were immediately lowered in an attempt to wedge the vessel off the reef, but no amount of heaving would move it. As the tide began to ebb, she settled more heavily upon the coral and was in danger of breaking up. The coast was 24 miles away and there was little hope of the ship's boats transporting all of the men ashore. Six cannons were thrown overboard, along with cannon balls, a quantity of iron and stone ballast, the fresh water and all of the casks containing decayed stores in an attempt to lighten the ship. The leaking hull remained fast and the ship's pumps could barely keep pace with the water flooding the hold. Twenty-three hours after first striking, the ship began to

A portrait of Captain James Cook by John Webber 1778.

move and within a few minutes they had hauled her into open water. After passing a spare sail under the hull to stem the leak, they managed to beach the ship in an estuary of a small river a few miles to the north. A camp was set up on shore and the damage was inspected. By chance, a large lump of coral had become lodged in the largest hole and this had prevented the ship from foundering at once.

During this period, the officers and men often went out and explored the Great Barrier Reef. The naturalist, Banks, was impressed with the abundance of tropical fish-life and seabirds, many of which were new to science. He described the reef as a 'wall of coral rock rising almost perpendicularly out of the unfathomable ocean'.

Compass from Cook's ship, the *Endeavour*, the first to successfully navigate the Great Barrier Reef.

The men, however, feared the reef. Crocodiles, huge sharks and the sharp fangs of the coral which could again rip the bottom of their ship were hazards they were not done with.

By 7 July, the major damage to the ship had been repaired and she was refloated. After reloading all of her stores they set sail on 4 August for the north. Then followed two weeks of complicated and dangerous sailing as Cook manoeuvered the ship through the labyrinth of coral reefs till, at last, on 21 August, they were around the tip of Cape York. Here, they paused at a small island, which they named Possession, and formally declared their discoveries by hoisting the Union Jack. Cook then claimed the eastern coast of the continent in the name of King George III.

On 28 April, 1789, just 15 months after the first Australian settlement was established at Port Jackson and only a few short months before the eruption of the French Revolution in Europe, Lieutenant William Bligh found himself and 18 others adrift in the Pacific in the launch of the *Bounty* — the result of the notorious mutiny. His 3618 nautical mile voyage in an open boat is unparalleled in the annals of seafaring. Having spent one month of desperate sailing during which one man was killed by hostile natives, Bligh sighted the Great Barrier Reef on 28 May. The following morning an opening through the barrier was found near Cape Direction and the launch was in the safety of calmer waters. Their immediate concern was food and a fresh supply of water whereupon they landed at a number of places as they continued along the coast toward the north. On 3 June they entered Cook's Endeavour Strait and by the evening were clear of the strait and on their way to safety at Coupang on the island of Timor.

Upon Bligh's eventual return to England the British Admiralty commissioned Captain Edward Edwards, commanding the 24-gun frigate *HMS Pandora*, to proceed to the South Pacific to apprehend the *Bounty* mutineers and bring them to justice. Fletcher Christian and eight of his accomplices had sailed *Bounty* to remote Pitcairn Island. The remaining 16 *Bounty* crew had elected to stay at Tahiti. By 23 March, 1791 when *Pandora* dropped anchor at Matavia Bay, only 14 remained alive.

The frigate *HMS Pandora* which had apprehended the mutineers from *HMS Bounty*, was itself wrecked on a reef north of Raine Island in 1791.

Six days later, and a few thousand miles away at Port Jackson, a small cutter departed in the early hours of the morning. On board were Mary Bryant, her husband William and two young children and seven others. They were convicts seeking desperately to escape the harsh conditions of the struggling settlement. Ten weeks and 3254 miles later, they had become the first Europeans to travel the entire eastern seaboard of Australia (Cook had sailed part of the distance outside of the Barrier Reef). Once they had arrived at Coupang, they represented themselves as shipwreck survivors. However, they were later found out and imprisoned.

Meanwhile Captain Edwards was rounding up the *Bounty* mutineers at Tahiti. A few of them had built a small schooner planning to attempt a voyage to the East Indies from whence they hoped to return to their native England. Edwards had the schooner refitted to serve as a support vessel during his search through the South Pacific for Christian and the other mutineers. At one of the islands, *Pandora* and the schooner were separated. Not being able to re-establish contact, Master's mate Oliver, Midshipman Renouard, and six seamen sailed the small schooner toward safety in the East Indies. Coming upon the Great Barrier Reef and not being able to find a passage through it, they boldly forced their way over the reef. Passing through Torres Strait, they eventually reached Samarang on the island of Java.

A gold watch owned by the ship's surgeon,
George Hamilton, recovered from the *Pandora*.

Edwards, on *Pandora*, searched the Pacific for nearly four months to no avail. Finally giving up, he turned towards England by way of the Strait. While searching for a new, more direct passage through the Barrier Reef, *Pandora* was wrecked on 29 August 1791 approximately 12 nautical miles north of Raine Island. Four mutineers and 31 of the crew were lost in the wreck. The 91 survivors sailed the ship's boat to Coupang where Edwards assumed the responsibility of transporting Mary Bryant and the other escaped convicts to England.

Divers working on the wreck of the *Pandora*.

After *Pandora* had sailed from England, William Bligh had been given another ship, *HMS Providence*, in which to complete *Bounty's* mission of collecting breadfruit plants for the West Indies. On board with Bligh was a bright young midshipman by the name of Matthew Flinders. After collecting the plants in Tahiti, Bligh, like Torres, approached the Strait at the northern end and passed the extremity of the outer barrier, sailed south-west and found a tortuous passage through the reefs and islands into the Arafura Sea.

During this period, most ships leaving Port Jackson were bound for India, China or the East Indies and sailed the long route east and north of New Guinea sometimes taking as long as six months. To use the short cut through the Torres Strait could save as much as 2000 miles but the Strait was regarded with scepticism and suspicion.

A barnacle-encrusted wine bottle from the wreck of the *Pandora*.

In 1793, Captain Bampton, of the brig *Shah Hormuzeer*, with a contract to bring supplies to the colony from India, decided to try the shorter route. Sailing in company with the British whaler *Chesterfield*, and with little knowledge of the reefs, he managed to cross the outer barrier and thread his way through taking 72 days.

At the turn of the century, the Admiralty recognised the need for better charts and sailing directions and commissioned Lieutenant Matthew Flinders in the *Investigator* to circumnavigate the Australian continent for this purpose. In 1802 he sought and found a way through the barrier and into Torres Strait. His transit took only five days and proved that a safe passage through the Strait was practicable.

On April 17, 1803, Captain Eber Bunker of the whaling ship *Albion* discovered and chartered the southernmost group of islands and reefs of the Barrier Reef. A note on his chart says — 'I sent two boats on shore which soon returned with 19 excellent turtles'. Today the group is known as the Capricorn-Bunker Group.

Later in 1803, Matthew Flinders, sailing as a passenger aboard *HMS Porpoise* on his way to England, planned to guide two merchant vessels, *Cato* and *Bridgewater*, through the Barrier Reef and Torres Strait. Unfortunately *Porpoise* and *Cato* discovered a new reef in the Coral Sea which is now called Wreck Reef as a result of their misfortune. Flinders, in command of one of the ship's boats, returned to Port Jackson for assistance. With three vessels, he sailed back to the reef where the survivors had established a camp on a small sand cay and subsequently continued his voyage in the 29-ton schooner *Cumberland*. He once more passed through the Barrier Reef and Torres Strait. Because of hostilities between Britain and France Flinders was arrested on arrival at Mauritius but after a prolonged internment eventually returned to England.

The skipper of the *Francis*, one of Flinders' rescue ships, was Captain James Aitken. Aitken returned to Wreck Reef in 1804 to salvage metal from the *Porpoise* and while there observed the potential of the reef for bêche-de-mer fishing. Taking samples back to Port Jackson he was successful in finding backers for his venture. Aitken thought none of the cays on Wreck Reef suitable as a base for his operation, so he set up a curing station on the southernmost island in the Bunker Group. Soon others followed and before long Wreck Reef was fished out. Other grounds were discovered in the more sheltered waters inside the barrier and gradually the fishermen worked their way up the coast thus establishing the first real industry of the Great Barrier Reef, an industry which would last for 100 years and would encourage the movement of Europeans into Queensland's far northern regions. The pioneers were a motley bunch of rogues and escaped convicts who, spurred on by the prospect of quick money, headed for the reef in anything that would float. They sailed into obscure places on the coast, worked reefs which bore no name and set up camps on sand cays which would disappear in the next heavy storm.

The use of the inner route to Torres Strait, between the coast and the barrier, was just beginning to be cautiously attempted by merchantmen. One of the first was Captain Cripps of the brig *Cyclops* bound for India from Port Jackson in 1812. The earliest ship known to have been wrecked inside the barrier was the 135-ton brig *Morning Star* in 1814.

The ship had sailed from Port Jackson for Batavia and Bengal in early July. Few records survive but from the position of her wreck it would appear that her master, Robert Smart, had sailed the outer route as far north as Cape Weymouth and then attempted to enter the reef at Quoin Island Entrance. Threading his way through the reefs of the uncharted waters, his passage to the clear inner route was blocked by the long hook-shaped Eel Reef. Steering north to round the obstruction, *Morning Star* struck a small isolated reef. The survivors managed to sail the ship's longboat to Booby Island at the western side of the Strait where five of the crew were rescued by the *Eliza* on 30 September. Smart and nine others had continued on to Timor in the longboat on the 25th.

Booby Island where the crew of the wrecked *Morning Star* survived for several weeks.

The following year *Eliza* herself was totally wrecked on the Barrier Reef and the survivors underwent a similar experience. A note saying that the crew had left the wreck in two boats was left under a flagstaff erected on an island in Endeavour Strait and was subsequently found by a passing ship. Both boats got safely over the reef and anchored in the lee of one of the Sir Charles Hardy Islands. Further particulars of the eventual fate of the survivors have not been found. The *Eliza* had been wrecked on 12 June. Only six days before, the brig *HM Kangaroo*, under the command of Lieutenant Charles Jefferies, rounded Cape York, having sailed and charted the inner route from Port Jackson.

In 1816 the ship *Lady Elliot*, sailing up the inner route, sighted one of Eber Bunker's islands where James Aitken had established his first bêche-de-mer curing station and named it after the ship. For many years historians have claimed that a wreck found in a creek near Cardwell was the *Lady Elliot*. It is now known that the ship was wrecked in 1823 off Point Palmiras. The identity of the Cardwell wreck remains a mystery.

In the 1800s a pearl shell industry developed in the Torres Straits.

The Barrier Reef claimed other victims. In 1817 the ship *Fame*, which had carried convicts to Port Jackson was wrecked while en route to Batavia. This was followed by the wreck of the *Frederick* in 1818.

The time was right to complete the coastal survey that Flinders had begun. The man chosen to undertake the work was Lieutenant Phillip Parker King. Governor Macquarie purchased the 84-ton, teak-built cutter *Mermaid* for the task and, after a surveying voyage to the north and north-west coasts of Tasmania, King sailed north from Port Jackson on 8 May 1819. It soon became apparent that many vessels were already using the inner route. Evidence was found that trees had been cut down to make large ship's spars which would find a ready market in other ports. On the northern tip of Stanley Island at the entrance to Princess Charlotte Bay, King found the remains of the *Frederick*. It had been reported that her captain and four of the crew had been rescued by another ship but what had become of the longboat with the remaining 23 was never discovered. Publication of Lieutenant Jefferies' journal of his survey of the inner route three years earlier had been supressed by Governor Macquarie due to a long-running disagreement between the two. King was to receive the major credit for compiling the survey data which led to the first comprehensive charts and sailing directions for the inner route. He became a strong advocate of the route and vigorously promoted its use.

There remained, however, the traditionally conservative shipmasters who were opposed firstly to the Torres Strait route because of the hazards of crossing the outer rim of the barrier if the outer route were used, and secondly to the inner route because it required the ships to anchor during the night which was both time

Post Office Cave, Booby Island, where supplies were stored for European shipwreck survivors.

consuming and tedious with the lightly-manned merchantmen. Eventually, the opposition lessened and both routes were used more and more frequently; however the outer passage was still favoured. The narrow and difficult openings through the barrier were often well marked by numerous wrecks sitting high and dry upon the reef. The gaps in the reef were difficult to locate from seaward as they were too far from land to allow accurate bearings to be taken. The prevailing winds and currents, the poor visibility caused by storms, and the lack of manoeuvrability of the cumbersome ships contributed to the seafarers' difficulties.

A contemporary painting of the *Doelwijk*, a Dutch vessel which was wrecked on Kenn Reef in 1854.

In 1837 the Admiralty dispatched *HMS Beagle* under Commander Wickham to begin an extensive 13 year survey programme aimed at improving shipping safety. Captain Blackwood in the corvette *Fly* and Lieutenant Yule in the tender *Bramble* continued the survey from 1841. Blackwood determined that the entrance through the reef at Raine Island was by far the best and in 1844 erected a stone tower as a beacon to mark the channel. Several wrecks had occurred in the vicinity prior to the beacon being built and more were to take place afterwards, but the frequency declined due to the prominent marker.

After having survived the extreme hardships of shipwreck, hunger and thirst, the crew's and passengers' trials were far from over. They were hundreds of miles from the nearest civilisation and some of the natives of the mainland and islands of the Strait were hostile and suspected to be cannibalistic and headhunters. A high proportion of shipwreck survivors did not survive the subsequent attempt to reach safety.

A place of refuge where one could safely await rescue was needed. Booby Island, a small cave-pocked rock at the western side of Torres Strait had been a haven for the men of the *Morning Star* in 1814. It was found to be a place avoided by islanders due to legends of evil spirits residing there. Soon, it became the traditional stopping place for vessels after the arduous passage through the Strait and the logical place for castaways to find shelter and eventual rescue. In a large cave near the landing place on the western end, supplies were stored for their benefit.

Subsequent wrecks gave the Barrier Reef a notoriety which was well deserved. It was an incredibly difficult piece of water to navigate because hidden dangers lurked only centimetres beneath the surface and many of them were still uncharted.

An effort to alleviate some of the problems of sanctuary for shipwreck survivors as well as establishing some modicum of presence within the area of the northern reaches of the Reef is reflected in the establishment of the tiny settlement of Somerset on the eastern side of the tip of Cape York.

A painting of a shipwreck on Friday Island in the Torres Strait, by the artist Isaac Jenner.

In 1863 Police Resident Frank Jardine arrived at the place selected and commenced to build a residence and outbuildings. The local Aborigines just to the south of the settlement were not altogether happy about this intrusion and continued to give Jardine trouble for some time. In any event, Jardine's Somerset became the haven of not only shipwreck survivors but was the intended coaling station for the new steam ships. Jardine also managed a bit of private enterprise by building up a fleet of small boats engaged in the bêche-de-mer trade. It is from the voyage of one of his tiny fleet that we have the only recorded incident of actual treasure being found on the Barrier Reef.

The story has several versions but the most widely accepted is that in 1889 Captain Samuel Roe of Jardine's schooner *Lancashire Lass* was returning from a voyage to the Coral Sea. During a gale, a freak wave lifted her over the edge of Boot Reef, near Murray Island, and dumped the boat into the relative safety of the lagoon. When the stormy seas subsided, the schooner was trapped and the only way out was to use crowbars to break a channel to open water. As the crew were breaking a large lump of coral, a mass of silver coins, blackened by long immersion in the sea, poured forth. They were Spanish Pieces of Eight or "dollars" dating from the early 1800s. These were the commonly accepted currency in the East Indies and were generally used in the early decades of the Australian settlement. Nearby were found an anchor and two cannons. The coins Roe handed over to Jardine were sufficient for a quantity to be made into a silver dinner service. Many were given away as souvenirs and the residue realised 3700 English pounds.

There are many tales of Spanish, Portuguese, Dutch, Chinese and even Egyptian wrecks occurring on the Barrier Reef. Invariably, as the tale goes, each and every one of these mythical ships had a hold laden with fabulous treasure. Undoubtedly, there are a few small treasures yet to be found on the reef. In 1826 the brig *Sun* was wrecked on the reefs called Eastern Fields. She supposedly carried between thirty and forty thousand Spanish dollars shipped by a Sydney merchant. Extant records do not mention whether the money was recovered.

Excavation of the wreck of the *Valetta* at Long Island in the Whitsundays.

Lady Elliot Island, one of the islands mined for guano in the 1860s.

A wreck at Long Island in the Whitsundays, long referred to as the "Spanish Galleon", was excavated in 1986 by the Queensland Museum and a group of volunteers. It has been proven to be the *Valetta*, a ship built of teak in Calcutta in 1821 and wrecked in 1825. Her only treasure had been bags of Newcastle coal.

Other industries began to develop on the Reef during the 1860s. The mining of guano or bird droppings which had accumulated for centuries was a profitable activity which thrived for a few decades. Lady Elliot Island in the Bunker Group, Bird Islet on Flinder's Wreck Reef, and Raine Island were the most productive but provided poor anchorages for the ships which called to load the bagged fertiliser. Several were wrecked at Bird and Lady Elliot when the wind direction changed and blew them ashore.

The 1860s also saw the advent of the sugar cane industry in central Queensland. In order to find a substantial labour force which could work in the fields under

This Solomon Islander is wearing a 'trade' armlet, part of his payment for work in the cane fields of North Queensland.

Trade goods, mainly armlets, found on the wreck of the *Foam*.

the fierce tropical sun, the plantation owners turned once again to the Pacific Islands. Islanders, mainly from the New Hebrides and the Solomons, were recruited for a government regulated period of three years. The kanakas, as they were called, were paid in trade goods to the value of three pounds per year. To them, this was a fortune. When they returned to their islands after the three year period, they had wealth and status within their own villages.

On an evening in 1893, the schooner *Foam*, while on a voyage to return 80 Solomon Islanders to their homes and to recruit new labour for the sugar fields, ran upon Myrmidon Reef, 75 nautical miles north-east of Townsville. No lives were lost but the ship was a total wreck and very little was saved. In 1982 the site of the wreck was rediscovered. Of greatest importance to the underwater archaeologist is the fine collection of trade goods found on the wreck. Certain of the items, such

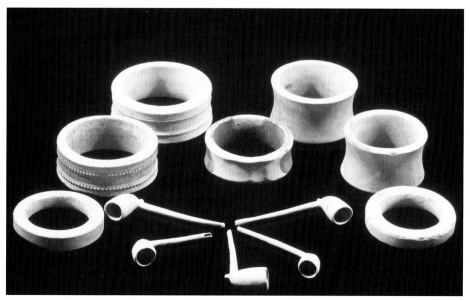

Examples of trade goods seen in the Queensland Museum.

58

This turtle shell was used by the survivors of the wreck of the *SS Gothenburg* to record their escape.

Some of the survivors of the *Gothenburg* pose for the camera.

as ceramic copies of traditional Pacific Islander shell armlets, were previously unrecorded and are of particular interest to anthropologists.

With the growing use of steam-powered vessels from the mid-nineteenth century and the discovery of gold and copper in central and northern Queensland, the ship traffic along the inner route increased tremendously. Also, steamships could navigate the Torres Strait from either direction unlike sailing ships which could not make the passage against prevailing winds. The route between the southern Australian settlements and China, the East Indies, and India was considerably shortened. But even the highly manoeuvrable steamships could be wrecked. In 1875 the South Australian government vessel *SS Gothenburg* was caught in a cyclone and totally wrecked on Old Reef south-east of Townsville. On a quiet moonlit night in 1890, *SS Quetta* struck an uncharted rock near Mount Adolphus Island at Cape York

An artist's impression of the *Gothenburg* shortly before she was wrecked on Old Reef near Townsville.

The *SS Yongala*, one of the most famous wrecks on the Barrier Reef and now a popular diving site.

and sank within three minutes. One hundred and thirty-three lives were lost. In 1911, *SS Yongala* was the victim of another cyclone and disappeared with 120 people. The wreck was rediscovered off Cape Bowling Green by a minesweeper during the Second World War. Today, the *Yongala* is one of the most popular wreck diving sites in the world and is visited by thousands of overseas tourists each year.

The Second World War brought with it the threat of enemy attack. Japanese aircraft bombed Horn Island in the Torres Strait and Japanese and German submarines were active off the Australian coastline attacking allied shipping. Several of the hundreds of passages through the Barrier Reef were mined in an attempt to reduce the threat of invasion by sea. Nonetheless, many unsubstantiated stories persist of secret landings on the Queensland coast and of sunken submarines inside the Barrier Reef.

After the War, the real invasion began — the tourism boom. Access to the Barrier Reef had increased with expanded airline facilities along the coast and Australians suddenly discovered the charm of a relaxing holiday under the palm

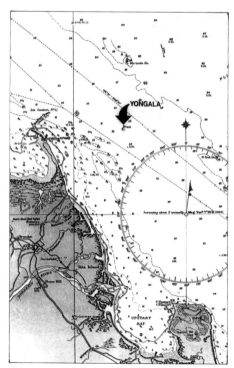

A chart showing the position of the wreck of the *Yongala*.

A member of the Queensland Museum staff examines an oyster-encrusted porthole from the *Yongala*.

The coral growth on the wreck of the *Yongala* greets the visitor with a blaze of colour.

trees of a tropical island. Lazy days of fishing, swimming, and exploring the fascinating coral reefs were an attraction few could resist. At first, the resort facilities were fairly basic but adequate. However, once Australia's Great Barrier Reef became a popular destination for wealthy overseas travellers, multi-million dollar resorts were built to attract the foreign tourists.

The Reef's unparalleled beauty, both below and above water, its diversity of unique marine life, its cultural resources such as Aboriginal sites and nearly 1500 historic shipwrecks, and its idyllic situation, are now protected. Australia's Great Barrier Reef is the largest marine park in the world. By intelligent regulation of its usage, future generations will always be able to enjoy and appreciate all it has to offer.

MARINE LIFE

LESTER CANNON

IMPRESSIONS of vivid colours — blue, turquoise, white, green, purple and blue again — and glare from an intense tropical sun greet the visitor to the Great Barrier Reef. The sea is a deep blue full of dancing glints and flecks of foam; the sky is a dome of blue, pale towards the horizon where clouds seem always to form an encircling line. It is hot, the air laden with salty moisture. The breeze brings smells of salt, of diesel and of fish. The throb of an engine or the slap of waves along the hull mark the passage of the boat; and nothing is still.

Morning calm. The world below will be stirring. New players for a new day.

As the boat nears the reef the sea changes to dark purple; there is a hint of brown where bommies nudge the surface and, beyond the crest of the reef where waves are thrown up, the shallowing water shades through turquoise to crystal clear. Here sand, nearly white in the bright sunlight, pulls out of the sea and is rimmed with foam. A low carpet of grass and vines binds the sand or vibrant green vegetation tops the cay. The sounds of breakers on beach and reef are but a rhythm above which can be heard the distant prattle of terns. A rich, pungent smell of rotting vegetation and guano catches the breeze.

Anchored off the reef. An ideal day for a reef walk.

Down below, beneath the water's surface, the coral reef lives and dies. For Dr John Veron, an authority on reef corals and a senior staff member of the Australian Institute of Marine Science (AIMS) in Townsville, the Reef generates a sense of 'wilderness, the feeling of open space, unexplored and largely unknown'.

Corals of every shape, spaces for every creature.

Plunging through the surface takes us from heat and glare into a cool and muted world. We are alone, invaders feeling excitement and often fear. As we begin to look out away from ourselves our calm returns. A large fish, curious, swims close to ogle the intruders, others dart or glide away matching speed and distance with the nature of our approach. Some seem content simply to ignore us.

Familiar noises are dulled — a wave, a motor — then as our senses adjust, sounds emerge, the clicking, popping and scraping noises of the Reef's inhabitants.

Visual impressions are strongest. On the beach it is birds, a turtle or the sun sinking behind a *Casuarina* tree. Below the water it is the shapes of the corals, the movements of the fishes and the dominance of blues tinged with green that we remember. Shafts of sunlight, bars of grey light radiating through the water, catch plankton in their beams like motes of dust floating through a chink of light in a darkened room.

One of the locals, a hussar, comes to check out the newcomer.

Sunlight scatters downward from that other world.

Swimming closer to the coral reveals the colours of the Reef. Never as bright as when caught in the photographer's flash, the reds, yellows, greens, blues, purples, browns, blacks and greys are all softened by increasing distance and depth.

Clarity of water can be outstanding with visibility in excess of 50m not uncommon on the outer reefs. Closer to the mainland or to an island or cay, nutrients from the surface, plankton in the water or sediments stirred up by currents and water movement can dramatically reduce this.

Everyone who explores the Great Barrier Reef recalls some intimate moment. Phil Alderslade, curator of soft corals at the Northern Territory Museum, remembers soft corals as 'green fields waving backwards and forwards like corn in the wind'. Many recall their first encounter with a shark or whale or just that first dive over the edge of the Reef's rim. Clives Jones, a biologist with the Queensland Fisheries, constantly relives 'the amazement and thrill of spilling a trawl net onto the sorting tray. Every catch reveals something new — to a marine biologist it's Christmas!'

To explore the Great Barrier Reef is to open a Pandora's box of sights, sounds and sensations. It is a world of colours and forms, still largely unexplored, yet as exciting and diverse as any we can imagine.

The butterfly cod, or lion fish, *Pterois volitans.*
Diaphonous fins belie their deadly stings.

Chaetodon ulientensis, an often solitary inhabitant of
the reef slopes.

The clown triggerfish, *Balistoides conspicillum,* will
use its powerful jaws to gnaw a retreat in the reef.

DIVERSITY characterizes the marine life of the Great Barrier Reef. There are hundreds of coral species, perhaps 2000 fishes, thousands of invertebrates and unknown numbers of microbes. These biological riches contrast with the paucity of life in the surrounding tropical seas which are poor in nutrients. This makes the Reef, in the words of Dr John Coll of James Cook University, seem 'like an oasis in the desert'.

Among the largest of the Reef's creatures, and certainly our closest relatives in the sea, are the mammals. Of the dozen or more whales and dolphins found in waters of the Reef, the best known are the humpback whale and the bottlenose dolphin. Humpbacks are baleen whales which leave their feeding grounds in the Antarctic each winter to breed in the Reef's warm waters. Unlike the humpbacks, the dolphins are toothed whales which feed on fish and squid and spend much of their time in waters close to shore.

The inshore regions, where seagrasses bind mud and sand, are home to the dugongs, the mermaids of legend. These ponderous creatures, unrelated to whales and dolphins, gather in herds to crop seagrasses with the aid of their great, fleshy, upper lips.

There are birds aplenty and turtles and sea snakes too, but it is among the fishes where the richness and diversity of life is most apparent. From only a few centimetres to many metres in size, long and thin, fat and round, flat or compressed, drab or gaudy, shy or bold, the fishes rule the reefs.

Boxfish, triggerfish and pufferfish set up territories on the reef flats. Schools of goatfish and flashing silver-biddies move over the sands; flatheads, flatfish and soles bury themselves, and wait for their prey. Damselfish form hovering clouds of colour, while gobies and blennies are ever quick to take cover.

Hidden among the corals, sponges and weeds are frogfish, scorpion fish and pipefish, all masters of disguise; and in darker crannies rest nocturnal squirrelfish, while eels lurk, mouths agape, at the entrance to a gloomy hole.

Like busy shoppers bold and colourful fishes crowd the reefs — the butterfly fish, the angelfish, fusiliers, wrasses and parrotfish, surgeonfish, rabbitfish, drummers, emperors, hussars and cods.

Masters of the open water, a pair of trevally, flash by.

The gaudy colours of the harlequin tuskfish, *Choerodon fasciatus,* are irresistible to the underwater photographer.

Canthigaster valentini is a common and pugnacious dweller of the reef flat.

Cruising off the reef are mackerels, trevally and long-toms and all the small fishes of open waters — herrings, anchovies, hardyheads. Closer to the surface and skimming for plankton are garfish or the extraordinary flying fish that can flick themselves out of water and glide across the waves.

Sharks are efficient predators and scavengers. They deserve respect, but not all are streamlined, grey and deadly like the hammerhead or the whalers. Carpet sharks or wobbegongs are most often encountered resting on the bottom in mottled disguise.

Juvenile batfish, *Platax pinnatus,* often swim on their sides.

A sea snake sculls over the reef seeking a meal.

A shovelnosed ray, *Rhynchobatus djiddensis*, rests in the sands of the lagoon.

Lagoon sands hide stingrays or elongate shovelnosed rays. Eagle rays with a pointed snout for digging prey from the sand make spectacular leaps from the sea and along the Reef's crest a lucky diver will encounter the giant manta scooping up the plankton upon which it feeds.

Ascidians live attached to the bottom (i.e. they are sessile); they occur singly or in colonies, and are often beautiful creatures. Though lacking a backbone, they are close relatives of the vertebrates.

Both beautiful and bizarre, the echinoderms are among the strangest of beasts. They have no head and tail, no dorsal and ventral, no left and right. These animals are radially symmetrical and their skin is filled with calcareous plates. They move with the aid of hundreds of tube feet controlled by a hydraulic system unknown in any other animal group.

We all know of the starfish, symbol of the sea shore, but on the Reef there are also brittlestars lurking under boulders, sea urchins burrowing into rocks, sea cucumbers shovelling up sediments and the most beautiful of all, the feather stars, perched on some prominence, their feathery arms gracefully curling as they filter their food from the sea.

A solitary ascidian. Close relative of the vertebrates, it lives permanently attached and filters its food from the water.

A cluster of delicate ascidians, tiny jewels living a protected life below a boulder.

A delicate fan of arms stretches out from the feather star to intercept food from the currents.

The spotted holothurian, or sea cucumber, is a soft bodied echinoderm, its spiny dermal plates reduced to tiny spicules.

The blue starfish, *Linkia laevigata*, is a conspicuous inhabitant of reef flats.

69

A typical marine snail or gastropod, the volute has a beautiful shell to protect its body.

This scallop, a bivalve mollusc, protects its delicate body with twin shells, each encrusted with other life.

The delicate nudibranchs have lost their shell. These snails with naked gills rely on colour for camouflage.

Molluscs are built to another plan. With more than 100 families and many thousands of species, they are among the most diverse of reef animals. Their body is muscular and equipped with a special area of tissue, the mantle, which secretes the shell. Shells may be heavy or light, plain or patterned, simple or complex. Toe-nail shells or chitons have a row of plates along their back; gastropods have one spiral shell into which their body can withdraw; bivalves have two shells which can close about the body; and cephalopods — squids, cuttlefish and octopus — have little or no shell at all.

The cephalopods have modified that other great molluscan structure, the foot, into an elaborate series of sucker-lined tentacles.

Perhaps the most successful body plan of all is that found among the crustaceans. Protection of soft body tissues is gained from their external skeleton of jointed plates.

Crabs protect their abdomens further by tucking them underneath them and hermit crabs borrow snails' shells; crayfish, shrimps and prawns use the powerful muscles of their abdomen for rapid escape; mantis shrimps have elaborate claws for grasping prey. Other crustaceans include the flattened isopods and compressed amphipods, while continually swimming in the water are shrimp-like mysids and microscopic copepods.

Then there are the worms — a polyglot lot. Zoologists recognize about 20 different phyla. This is diversity indeed, for the fishes, reptiles, birds and mammals comprise but part of one phylum — the chordates.

A tiny crab clambers over soft coral.

A delicate morsel for some passing fish, this shrimp rests on a purple sponge, ready for instant escape.

The delicate whorls of the feeding tentacles of the fan worm, *Spirobranchus giganteus*, jut from a protected home in a coral.

The most conspicuous worms are the polychaete annelids with an elongate body divided into rings each armed with numerous small spines or chaetae. Tufts of feeding tentacles of the tube dwelling or sedentary polychaetes sprout from many a coral bommie. Wandering polychaetes like to burrow in sand or crawl into crevices.

Robust spoon worms draw in food with a trough-like pharynx, peanut worms hide below rocks, ribbon worms slide and slime after their prey and polyclad worms, paper thin and often brilliantly coloured, are so incredibly delicate that they seem to seep over the surface of rocks.

Microscopic worms live between the grains in sands and sediments, and there are parasitic worms — flukes, tapeworms, roundworms and others — living inside or on their hosts. It is estimated that for every species of free living animal several parasites exist. The numbers must be prodigious!

The hard corals, about 350 species, are the dominant life form on the Reef. Hard corals consist of small, simple animals, the polyps, which are joined together with common tissue to form colonies. The living tissue is but a thin veneer above a massive calcium carbonate skeleton. Each polyp is like a tiny bucket rimmed with six tentacles (or some multiple of six). The tentacles are covered with batteries of stinging cells, the nematocysts, with which the corals catch their prey.

The mushroom coral, *Fungia fungites*, is one of the few solitary corals and one that lives unattached to the reef.

Sponges are strange animals. Permanently attached and of simple construction, they add exciting colour and form to the reef.

Reef building or hermatypic corals have algae, the zooxanthellae, living in their tissues. These algae are able to capture sunlight, photosynthesize and so fix carbon. They use the corals' metabolic wastes and provide energy to aid in calcification and the construction of massive skeletons. Some corals, the ahermatypic ones, lack these algae and though they still form skeletons they do so much more slowly. They are smaller corals often living in darkened areas such as caves or deep water.

Soft corals do not build massive skeletons, though substantial skeletons may be created by sea fans and *Tubipora*, the organ-pipe coral, with its deep red skeleton. Anemones do not build skeletons either, but sometimes grow to a large size and zoanthids such as *Protopalythoa* can form leathery mats at the Reef's crest.

Corals have other relatives, the colonial hydroids found attached to the bottom and the scyphozoa, jellyfishes that float free in the water. Hydroid colonies may be tiny, delicate and feathery, or robust as in the case of the stinging hydroid *Aglaeophenia*, or even heavy and stony in the fire coral *Millepora*. Some hydroids such as the Portuguese Man-o'-War, *Physalia*, have floating colonies.

This beautiful needle coral, *Seriatopora hystrix*, will grow tall and fine in a protected environment, but the branches will be shorter and thicker where wave action is great.

Sponges live attached to the bottom. These simple animals feed by filtering. The body consists of numerous small chambers into which water is drawn through many tiny pores on the sponge's surface. After food is extracted in the chambers, water passes to larger chambers and then out via a few large pores. To support their many-chambered body sponges have protein skeletons to which they often add mineral spicules (especially of calcium carbonate) or particles of sand and shell. Sponges are multicoloured and multiformed; they may be encrusting or erect, spindly or robust, soft or firm.

Finally amongst the animals are the single celled protozoans. Many are parasitic, nearly all are microscopic. Larger ones called forams have tiny calcareous skeletons which are often seen as stars or punctured medallions on algal fronds. Their skeletons make up a great deal of the sand of a coral cay.

ANGELS OF THE REEF

To an underwater photographer there is an endless beauty to a coral reef. There is the supreme brilliance of the light in the water, the myriad of marine life of almost endless variety . . . the swish of the tail of a white-tip reef shark as it slinks by.

Yet some experiences are more memorable than others; dives can become events by virtue of one particular moment such as the excitement of observing a new species. On the Great Barrier Reef an encounter with one of the angelfish, a group of fish whose hallmarks are often an extraordinary colouration and a small spike extending backwards from their gill slits can live in the mind forever. However it is not just the distinguishing features of the group that make them remarkable.

It is the way that they move which is so beautiful. The larger members of the group glide through the water with almost surreal elegance, a profound effortlessness. They turn in front of the photographer in a tantalising fashion with a sense of calm and decision, unlike, for example, the butterfly fish which are always in a hurry.

Amongst the most beautiful of the angels of the reef are the blue angelfish, the navarchus angelfish, the six-banded angelfish and the common regal angelfish. The yellow-faced angelfish is an uncommon inhabitant of the reef and generally timid and unapproachable. On the basis of pure elegance and majesty however, the imperial angelfish *(Pomacanthus imperator)* must surely be the most dramatic, with its mask and complex horizontal bands in vivid blue and yellow. It is very much the sovereign of the reef.

Navarchus angelfish, *Euxiphipops navarchus*

Imperial angelfish, *Pomacanthus imperator*

Six-banded angelfish, *Euxiphipops sexstriatus*   Yellow-faced angelfish, *Euxiphipops xanthometapon*   Regal angelfish, *Pygoplites diacanthus*

The brilliant green of turtle weed, *Chloredesmis fastigiata*, is a common sight in the reef flat and upper slope.

The single cell of *Valonia* is mainly a big vacuole filled with fluid. The algal cytoplasm is stretched around it.

The plants are a vital part of any coral reef. On the inshore reefs of the north, mangrove trees grow on the cays, and wherever shallow sandy areas abound seagrasses are abundant. Most marine plants, however, are algae. Scattered in the waters single-celled phytoplankters such as dinoflagellates occur in countless numbers. In contrast, *Valonia*, though single celled, is as big as a golf ball. Brown, red and green algae, notably *Halimeda*, are also common.

Halimeda are algae which incorporate large plates of calcium in their tissues. In places much of the sand is made up from these plates.

76

Zooxanthellae, coralline and blue-green algae are vital to the Reef. Zooxanthellae are the algae which live inside the tissues of hard corals and some other creatures such as the giant clams, *Tridacna*. The coralline algae, like the corals, incorporate calcium into themselves to form hard, rocky structures. They may cement coral rubble or reef rim into a solid wall. The blue-green algae are the most important primary producers upon which the grazing and browsing herbivores of the Reef rely.

Why should there be such diversity of life on the Great Barrier Reef? Professor Joe Connell of the University of California, one of the world's leading coral reef ecologists, thinks it is because 'periodic small scale disturbance keeps the competitively dominant species from eliminating others'.

The Reef is a structural mosaic and chance plays a hand in creating this wondrous place. It is a treasure trove of genetic riches and each organism survives with its unique adaptations to life.

Caulastrea fuscata. Individual polyps retracted into their skeletons still reveal the greens and browns of the zooxanthellae embedded in their tissues.

ADAPTATIONS to life of the Great Barrier Reef, as to any watery medium, offer many advantages over a land-based existence. Dehydration is not a problem, for example, and a tough outer skin to keep in moisture is redundant. Animals and plants on the Reef can be very delicate with soft membranes through which gases and salts pass easily. Furthermore, the water itself provides support. Anyone who has seen an octopus or a jellyfish out of water can attest to the debilitating influences of gravity.

Animals need oxygen to burn their food and so build their tissues. Sea creatures, other than the air breathing vertebrates, live with oxygen levels in the ocean which are some 30 times less than in air. Tiny creatures with a large surface to volume ratio and with moist skins and delicate bodies may simply absorb oxygen through their skin, but larger animals need gills or similar structures.

One of the most extraordinary forms of gill is found in sea cucumbers. Just inside the anus sprouts a system of branching tubules, the respiratory trees, which extend into the body. Sea cucumbers breathe by pumping water in and out of these via their anus.

Water in the sea is in perpetual motion. It is much denser than air and takes a great deal of energy to resist. Soft bodies can be vulnerable; some form of skeleton

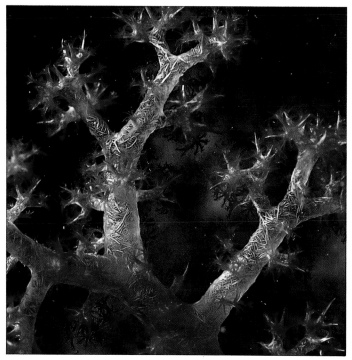

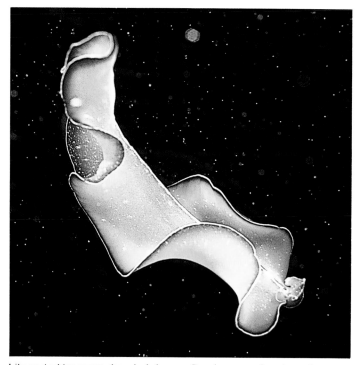

The reduced spicule skeleton of this soft coral, *Dendronephthya,* are evident through the transparent stem.

Like an Arabian carpet, the polyclad worm, *Pseudoceros,* swims sinuously through the water.

or heavy, outer shell provides protection. Skeletons are inside fishes, outside crustaceans and in the skin of echinoderms. Skeletons are solid in hard corals, but are made up of numerous, tiny spicules in many sponges and soft corals. In molluscs they can be inside cuttlefish, outside clams and snails or, as with nudibranchs, not there at all.

Skeletons grow as the animal grows. New coral polyps lay down their skeletons on the skeletons of older polyps. Soft corals, sponges and echinoderms add spicules and plates to support newly-developed soft tissues. As molluscs get bigger they add little by little more around the edges of their shells. Crustaceans, however, have their skeleton outside and so must cast off the old skeleton to grow. While their new shell is soft they pump themselves up with water to increase their size. They are most vulnerable to predation at this time.

A painted cray, *Panulirus versicolor*, lacks the large chelae or nippers of the related lobsters.

Skeletons are also important for locomotion for muscles act better with something solid to pull against. Many small, soft animals fill themselves up with water until their bodies are turgid. This provides a hydrostatic 'skeleton' to assist muscular action.

Getting about or swimming in water requires fins, flippers, flaps, a sinuous body motion or, in the case of squid, jet propulsion. Those animals that climb around the bottom use legs or a muscular gliding foot or, the most bizarre of all, rows of tube feet.

The water vascular system of echinoderms which controls the tube feet works by water being drawn into a closed system of tubes and reservoirs to maintain a high internal pressure. With the aid of muscles contracting and relaxing against this pressure, tube feet extend, suck on to a substrate and then shorten. This action draws the animals along like little wind-up toys.

The spider shell, *Lamblis lamblis*, is protected by a heavy calcareous skeleton – dull above, beautiful below.

Part of the remarkable water vascular system, the tube feet of a starfish extend and contract to propel the animal over the reef.

A spider shell from below. A pair of eyes peek out from the protective shell.

Sunlight, although little is reflected in the tropics, does not penetrate far into water. Within 10m less than 10% of the light intensity remains and by 20m this has fallen to less than 4%. Furthermore, about 40% of the red wave lengths are absorbed in 1m, but less than 5% of the blue-greens making these colours more evident. Colours, however, are among the most important adaptations of reef animals allowing them to exhibit species distinct patterns for recognition during courting or, alternatively, to camouflage themselves from predators.

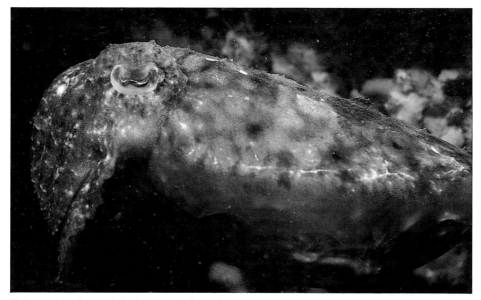

Cephalopods such as cuttlefish have especially sophisticated eyes. Undoubtedly their acuity aids animals in controlling the pigment cells in their bodies to achieve remarkable pattern changes and camouflage.

Nevertheless, sensitivity to light is of great significance in the clear waters of the Reef. Corals know when darkness falls, and, although echinoderms do not have eyes, they do have light sensitive spots (e.g. on the tips of starfish arms). Many molluscs have remarkable eyes: strombs have large, unblinking, stalked eyes and scallops have rows of small eyes which allow them to sense the shadow of a predator and flap away to safety. Octopus and squid have eyes functionally as good as the vertebrate eyes of fish. Crustacean eyes, like those of insects, are compound. They form mostly poor images, but are extremely good at sensing motion.

Sounds are important too for the Reef is a noisy place. Sound travels at about 1600m a second in tropical waters and the long, low wavelengths carry best. These are the carriers of the haunting songs of the humpback whales. Down among the corals little snapping shrimps stun their prey with the click of an enlarged claw. Fish can sense such vibrations through their lateral line system, a system of pressure sensitive cells along the head and sides.

The study of smells is difficult. We know that for most creatures of the Reef finding the correct habitat depends upon responding to the right set of chemical cues.

One notable adaptation discovered recently on the Reef is the ability of many corals, and some other invertebrates, to protect themselves from the harsh ultra-violet light of the tropics. Many of these animals have transparent tissues allowing passage of sunlight to their symbiotic algae. Special chemical blockers are developed which screen out the dangerous wavelengths, but do not impede those needed for photosynthesis.

Coloniality, however, may be of greatest significance. A watery medium brings food to sessile creatures. Where one survives, another may do so too. By developing colonies organisms both occupy space and also create more spaces. Judging from its common occurrence, coloniality has proven a profitable mode of life on the Great Barrier Reef. It is this adaptation, combined with the ability to incorporate calcium and make heavy skeletons, which has created the Great Barrier Reef itself.

Finally there are adaptations allowing animals to float and swim more easily. Many small creatures use gas bubbles to float at the surface. *Physalia*, the Portuguese Man-o'-War, has one of the individual polyps of the colony modified into a gas-filled sail and the snail *Janthina* traps bubbles in mucus. Small crustaceans gain buoyancy by storing oil droplets from their food and most marine fishes have closed swim bladders to help them maintain buoyancy. Bodies are also extended with folds, flaps and fins. These structures, especially in the young, allow the animal to float or to swim and be dispersed in the plankton.

PLANKTON is that drifting flora and fauna that for some is all of life, for others just a passing phase. To many it simply means food. It has been called a 'life sustaining soup' or 'the grass roots of the marine ecosystem'.

Within the permanent plankton are plants, the phytoplankton, and animals, the zooplankton. The plants are the primary producers, capturing the light of the sun and, with the aid of their chlorophyll, producing sugars and oxygen. Among the phytoplankton are diatoms, coccolithophores, blue-green algae and delicate dinoflagellates. The blue-green alga *Oscillatoria erythraeum* is noted for producing huge, brown windrows, like oily trails, which from time to time streak the seas of the Great Barrier Reef. Their millions and millions of rotting bodies can clog fish gills and pollute beaches.

Feeding on the plants are the zooplankters. The tiny crustaceans called copepods are the most common, but floating molluscs, jellyfish (large and small), voracious arrow worms, salps and siphonophores all make a permanent home in the plankton.

Although adrift these animals are not without swimming ability — feeble as it might be in relation to currents. Free swimming predators abound in the surface waters during the day, but most zooplankters swim down to deeper, darker water or seek shelter close to the bottom of the reef. When darkness comes, the corals feed and the zooplankters return to the surface waters where, in relative safety, they can feed on phytoplankton — and on one another.

An *Acropora* colony bursts forth with spawn.

As the full moon of early summer begins to wane a remarkable explosion of life takes place in the warming waters of the Great Barrier Reef. The corals spawn. More than 130 species of hard and soft corals are now known to pour their sex products into the sea in one short-lived, orgiastic release. For months the eggs have been ripening and the sperm maturing within their parent polyps. Some polyps, such as those of the mushroom corals, are either male or female, but most corals are hermaphrodites which release bundles containing both eggs and sperm. Bundles of pink, white, yellow, blue and green emerge one by one or virtually simultaneously over the whole colony. They float up, break and the sperms seek out their own kind while fishes dart and dive to gorge themselves till distended.

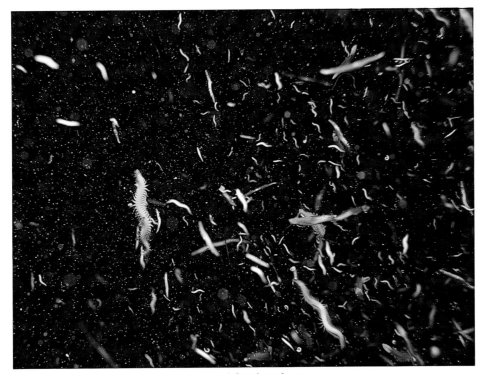

The waters fill with spawn from corals and worms. A feast is set for many.

The whole event lasts only a few days. It has been suggested the synchronism serves to swamp predators or to maximize cross fertilization. Perhaps it is accidental for even those same species of corals that spawn together on the Reef do not always do so in other regions of the world where temperatures and tides fluctuate less.

The union of sperm and egg produces a tiny ciliated larva, the planula, which is subject to the vagaries of the currents and carried away. The young planula develops, and soon moves towards the bottom to seek a safe and secure place to settle, to attach and to metamorphose into a tiny polyp and thus renew the cycle of growth.

Coral planulae are the temporary or 'new plankton', as are all the myriads of immature stages of the larger organisms which take advantage of the water, its buoyancy and its currents, to drift away and disperse.

A baby cephalopod, part of the temporary plankton, with a hazardous life ahead.

To become a temporary member of a different community, with different requirements, means that animals must change their form and behaviour — not once, but two or more times. Polymorphic life cycles (i.e. those with many life forms) are found in many reef animals. The sexual stages — eggs and sperm — of corals are formed within the sessile colony; but in the closely related, fern-like hydroids, tiny medusae (jellyfish) are released from the colony to form part of the plankton. It is in this stage that their eggs and sperm are produced.

Polychaete worms can produce tiny larvae called trochophores; molluscs produce trochophores and also veligers. These larvae are small, ciliated and largely transparent. Several different larval stages with jointed limbs (e.g. nauplius, zoea, phyllosoma) are recognizable as crustacean, but the larvae of echinoderms known as pluteus, auricularia and bipinnaria, were known from the plankton long before their echinoderm affinities were recognized.

Polymorphic life cycles have one common thread. Immature or larval forms must eventually return to that of the adult — they must undergo metamorphosis. This can occur while the larvae are still in the plankton, as happens with sea cucumbers, but most animals settle before they undergo the transformation to the adult's shape.

Settlement may take place within a few minutes or hours of the larvae or young entering the plankton; this means some young settle near the parent in favourable local conditions. Alternatively settlement may be delayed for weeks or even months while currents carry the young to far-off places and sometimes, because of the complexity of currents on the Reef, back again.

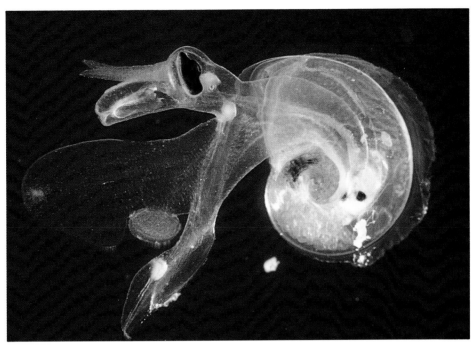

The pteropod snail is a member of the permanent plankton, its whole life spent drifting, swimming and feeding in open water.

Experiments on Helix reef in the central Great Barrier Reef have shown that more than 50% of larvae are retained in that reef's system. It seems that most dispersed young stay close to the parents. Nevertheless, young of sessile and sedentary animals must change from a planktonic life to one on the sea floor. It is essential they change their behaviour to seek the bottom and to settle quickly and safely if they are to colonize new habitats.

A larval mantis shrimp swims in the temporary plankton. It is specialised for this floating life and looks quite unlike the adult which will live burrowing on the reef floor.

A sea fan grows across the current making a net to catch its food.

HABITAT is a place to live. The Great Barrier Reef is like an enormous metropolis. The whole province encompasses the area of reefs and the seas between them from the coast to the edge of the continental shelf (i.e. waters of less than 100 fathoms). Living there are animals floating free or planktonic, those that are nektonic (swimming freely) or benthic (associated with the bottom). More particularly we can consider them in regard to where they live — between coral reefs, on reef slopes, reef flats or in lagoons.

The regions between the reefs are not well known. From sediment sampling we know that inner regions of the Reef are rich in silty deposits washed out from the mainland. Outer regions are almost entirely made up of coral particles. Surprisingly the fauna between the reefs over the whole of the continental shelf region is fairly homogeneous. Although there are creatures found only in turbid and silty inshore regions and others found only in clearer, oceanic realms near the shelf edge, most of this region has a similar suite of animals. It is the relative proportions which change. Corals, which are characteristic of reefs, are known to occur also in deeper water well away from the emergent or near-emergent reefs.

Research carried out at the Australian Institute of Marine Science has demonstrated a similar homogeneity across the reefs. There are more sponges inshore and algal diversity is highest offshore, but the changes are gradual across the continental shelf.

In both areas, between the reefs and on them, the Great Barrier Reef can be roughly divided into three regions, inshore, mid-reef and offshore. The distribution of fishes also shows this pattern. Because of the differences in width and strength of the coral barrier, the flow of oceanic water across the reefs is much less in the north where the ribbon reefs form a rampart. Here the mid-reef region is virtually non-existent and the inshore fauna extend across almost to the outer barrier.

A quiet spot on the reef – a large brain coral and spidery branches of staghorn corals.

Plate and staghorn *Acropora* are commonly found on the upper reef slope.

Under a ledge or in cover, out of the light, the yellow dendrophyllid corals thrive.

The most profuse coral growth occurs on reef slopes especially in the upper 30m. In deeper water sea whips, black corals and fan gorgonians live as well as some large brain corals. The deeper slopes sprout huge vase corals and soft corals while nearer the surface both plate and staghorn *Acropora* are found mingling with ever more diverse assemblages.

Under ledges along the reef slope live a wealth of hydroids, sponges and ahermatypic corals such as the yellow *Tubastrea*. Starfish, notably the large *Acanthaster planci*, also live there; and in sandy patches are found big sea cucumbers, which in earlier times were dried to make trepang, much prized in China.

Reef slopes are sometimes deeply cleft, providing habitats at a variety of depths.

A school of lightning predators, barracuda, gather off the reef edge.

The crinoids or feather stars are numerous and can be seen straining against the current. Shrimps and painted lobsters live in crevices. Sharks cruise, or rest on sandy patches between the corals, sea snakes nose about nooks and crannies, while turtles scull quietly away into the blue.

Large and small carnivorous fishes hunt on these slopes, with bottom feeders farther down. Herbivores and plankton feeders (planktivores) live nearer the surface where they can form prey for large carnivores such as the cods.

Beneath some shaded overhang a soft coral thrives.

These fish, *Heniochus acuminatus*, with their long trailing dorsal fins, are usually found in pairs.

No two reef slopes are alike. They may drop precipitously in a multitude of plate and branching corals or be deeply channelled with spurs of corals interchanging with sandy canyons. They may be a maze of boulders and debris with only tiny coral colonies in sheltered spots, or a sloping thicket of tall *Acropora*, or even a mixture of sand and bommies which drop off deeper and deeper.

Coral trout, *Plectropoma leopardus*, here showing a patchy colouration, are one of the most conspicuous large predators along the reef slopes.

90

Great plates of *Acropora* grow close to the reef crest where water is clean and sunlight is strong.

The crest of the reef faces the full force of the waves. A place of turbulence.

The windward slopes (i.e. usually south-eastern ones because of the prevailing trade winds) are steeper and covered with more rubble near the bottom. The richest coral growth occurs on these slopes near, yet just out of, the full force of the waves. To the lee (north-west) of the reef sand increases in abundance and coral patches are more isolated. The entire reef slope is a world of ceaseless movement. Continual surging of waves together with the ebb and flow of tides all take their toll as new growth crumbles to the base of the reef, ever adding to the limestone foundations.

Lagoons along the Reef are really no more than enclosed regions of leeward coral slope. Cuspate or C-shaped reefs have gradually closed to form lagoons and in some cases cays. Sometimes a reef is broken up into a ragged series of patch reefs. Lagoons offer quieter, more murky conditions.

Many of the corals and anemones from the slope also live in lagoons, but sand dwelling bivalves, gastropods, swimming crabs and prawns, starfish, heart urchins and many sea cucumbers occur most abundantly.

There are also turtles and many fishes, such as rays and flatfish, which bury in the sand; silvery mullets, emperors, goatfish and gerrids glean the sands for molluscs, crustaceans and worms. Herbivorous parrotfish and surgeon fish form gently moving schools, and among the coral outcrops damselfish, butterfly fish, wrasses and angelfish can be seen.

Between the reef slope and the lagoon lies the reef flat. It is this region of the reef which most casual visitors come to know best. The reef flat may be exposed at low tide or, as happens in many reefs of the central and northern area, it remains covered. On exposed reef flats coral colonies rise perhaps only 0.5m from the sand. These may form flat-topped microatolls where polyps grow around the sides and are prevented from doing so on top because of exposure. Reef flats may have a rich coral diversity, but it is in this area that the algae predominate.

Hiding below the reef slope, the flathead waits for some unwary prey.

Sea cucumbers such as this 'curry fish' pass large quantities of sand through themselves. This action continually disturbs the sediments.

Apart from the corals the most conspicuous invertebrates on reef flats are the giant clams, *Tridacna*, with their multi-hued mantles exposed to the sunlight, and sea cucumbers inexorably moving the sediments through their bodies.

The fishes of the region are mostly small, resident species — wrasses, gobies, blennies, boxfish, puffers and the brilliant little damselfish; but, on a rising tide, larger fishes swim over the reef flat — sharks, sweetlips, cods — as well as roving schools of parrotfish.

The reef flat may have deep pools left by an outgoing tide. These form microcosms of the reef and are alive with small fishes, corals and other invertebrates protected from both the physical violence of the reef slope and the hazard of predators.

Towards the rim of the reef flat, before it drops away down the slope, corals and calcareous algae grow more compactly and can form a pavement firm to walk on, yet honeycombed below and, at times, treacherous. Here little can grow erect: it is here where calcifying algae are abundant and where they cement the crest into a bulwark against the sea.

This region may be strewn with coral rocks. The sanctuaries in this habitat are the quiet places below the boulders where sponges, hydroids, lace-corals and ascidians abound and small molluscs, crustaceans, worms and echinoderms all live in bewildering variety.

The original owner of this turban shell is gone. Hermit crabs have a soft, vulnerable abdomen which they protect within a discarded shell.

Below boulders in sheltered spaces delicate 'lace corals', bryozoans, are able to build their fragile colonies.

Finally, whereas mangrove forests along the coast are often characterized by dark, putrescent mud, those on the inshore cays of the north usually grow in cleaner sediments. These shallow, intertidal habitats may have adjacent seagrass beds.

Here can be found the delectable mud crabs *Scylla serrata* and the gentle dugong, favourite foods of the coastal Aborigines. Among the prop roots of the mangroves the upside-down jellyfish, *Cassiopeia*, exposes its underside to the sun for the benefit of its symbiotic algae.

The Reef offers space for the sessile and the sedentary and places for the territorial and the wandering. In quiet, sheltered areas corals and sponges may grow tall and delicately branching while in regions of turbulence the same species becomes low and compact. 'It is a tropical system with great structural variation', says Dr J Baker, Director of AIMS, 'habitats of all types . . . and at temperatures optimal for life and reproduction'.

FOOD is the fuel for life. Ultimately all energy comes from the sun. The materials which make up the living veneer of the Reef and which can be found in its surrounding waters do not come from some external source, but are continually being recycled within the system. Nutrients, matter and energy in the system are passed from one organism to another. Structures are built up (i.e. reassembled from the basic chemicals of life) and torn down or disassembled for use in other ways.

This nutrient cycle begins with photosynthesis in the plants of the Reef — the zooxanthellae, those in the plankton and those attached to the ocean floor. These are the autotrophs or self-feeders which use the sun's energy to build from inorganic materials (e.g. calcium, carbon and oxygen) those chemicals that can be used by others, the heterotrophs (i.e. the microbes and animals).

Animals which eat plants are herbivores, those which eat other animals are carnivores and those which eat both are omnivores. Nutrients are passed from one to the other up the food chain, from primary producers, the plants, through the various consumer levels until they reach the top predators (e.g. sharks, sea eagles).

Soft coral polyps clutch at passing food.

A giant clam, *Tridacna*, exposes its broad mantle, filled with zooxanthellae, to the sunlight.

Peer in through the expanded syphon of the giant clam and the food gathering gills are revealed.

Parasites and scavengers divert nutrients and detritovores feed on detritus — the decomposing organic material which continually falls into and enriches the sands and sediments.

The Reef is a sea of mouths but a sedentary life can be most successful for the waters are filled with plankton. All that remains is to capture it and sedentary animals do this in an amazing variety of ways.

The commonest way, and one of the most efficient, is to pump water in, filter out the plankton, and return the water to the sea. Sponges do this; so do bivalve molluscs and ascidians. Sponges are simple animals, mere chambers lined with tiny cells that individually capture food particles. Bivalves and ascidians trap food on a tissue net and pass it in a ropy string of mucus to their mouths. Feeding on mucus is a speciality of reef animals, especially the small crabs that live with many corals.

Lying below the sediments some worms and short-spined sea urchins also draw in water to filter food. Relatives of the sea urchins, feather stars, some brittle stars and the sea cucumbers with branched tentacles, trap food in mucus nets spread on or between their arms or tentacles. All these animals are sedentary in habit, capable of moving, but often not doing so.

A sponge, through multiple pores, draws in water from which it extracts its planktonic food.

Clusters of solitary ascidians filter food from the seas. Their enormous filtering rate means they are able to capture enough food from the relatively nutrient poor reef waters.

At the other end of the scale are the huge filter feeders that cruise through the seas. Manta rays and basking sharks swim open-mouthed through the water and catch food on the rake-like projections in front of the gills.

Baleen whales take huge mouthfuls of water filled with plankton, and with enormous tongues they press out the water through rows of large hair-fringed plates, the baleen. Humpback whales do not feed in waters of the Reef because plankton is sparse in open tropical seas. Bryde's whale, however, lives all its life in warm waters and feeds by scooping up shoals of small fish.

There are even filterers of plankton that are themselves plankton. Salps are floating cousins to the ascidians, and the rhizostome jellyfishes have four trunk-like oral tentacles covered with tiny pores through which they sieve their food.

Filtering its food from the sea water, the giant manta ray, *Manta alfredi*, cruises through the water with accompanying remora attached.

A feather-duster worm, *Spirobranchus*, spreads its whorls of tentacles to trap a passing morsel.

Casting a net or setting a trap is another way that sedentary or slow-moving animals may capture their food. Slowly unfurling its brilliantly coloured tentacles from its protective home in a coral bommie the polychaete worm, *Spirobranchus*, waits for the touch of prey and withdraws with lightning speed. A hermit crab protecting its soft abdomen in a hole in the coral, rather than a more customary shell, will spread its finely-tufted antennae in the water and wait; while a barnacle similarly buried in coral, but this time head first, combs the water with its hairy legs in search of food.

A different kind of trap is set by the terebellid tube worm, *Reteterebella*, which sends out, across the sand and rubble, long, snaking, white tentacles from its home beneath a protective boulder.

Fishes too may hide in waiting: an eel hidden in a crevice, a scorpaenid camouflaged and deadly may strike too fast to be seen.

The yellow trumpet fish uses the bulk of the cruising coral trout to disguise its presence. At an appropriate moment it will peel off and strike.

Even some of the slow moving cone shells can bring down an unsuspecting fish. The radula of cone shells is reduced so that individual teeth are stored in a sac. Each tooth is hollow and packed with poison. Like a wary Amazonian hunter armed with his blow pipe the cone will stretch out its siphon, shoot out a deadly dart, and glide slowly to its stricken victim.

As on land, the sea has its grazing animals which feed on plants with little discrimination. Teeth or jaws of some gastropod molluscs or sea urchins rasp away at thin, algal turf and often substantially erode the underlying coral rock. Even in areas of apparently dead coral and rubble a profuse turf of blue-green algae provides a major source of food for herbivores on the Reef.

Parrotfish are browsers, they feed more selectively. Multi-species schools can be seen, and heard, moving slowly across the Reef pausing here and there to scrape away at the algal-covered rock with their large, fused teeth. Cascades of sandy faeces trail behind them.

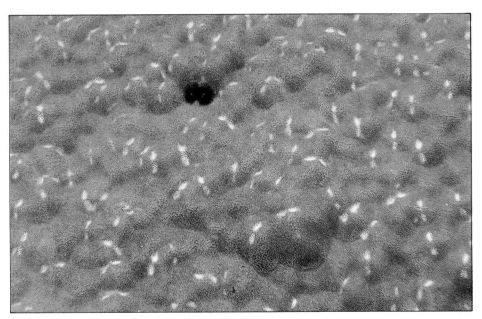

Paired scars on the coral signify a school of parrotfish have been here.

Wrasses are often confused with the parrotfish because of their size, shape and colours, but wrasses are predators with sharp, pointed teeth. They feed on a variety of small creatures, worms, crustaceans and molluscs.

Predators abound on the reefs. Corals and their relatives are predators. Each hungry mouth is ringed with tentacles ready to wrap their prey in a poisonous embrace. Polyclad flatworms and nudibranch molluscs glide over colonies of ascidians and lace-corals where they pluck out individuals one by one.

There are nudibranchs that can consume coral tissues, zooxanthellae and stinging cells. They digest the first, store and use the second, and incorporate the third into their skin in special folds, the cerata, for use in their own defence.

A chaetodon nips at coral polyps along the edge of the colony.

Jaws that grasp and jaws that chew are found in worms, crustaceans and fishes. Butterfly fish have long, pointed snouts to let them nip at coral polyps or reach into cracks and crannies for the creatures hidden there. Some predatory fishes such as sea-perch puff at the sediments to reveal their prey. Many of the bigger fishes (cods, trevally, mackerel and sharks) catch and eat fish — the old, young, infirm and unwary.

A predatory shark patrols.

The crown-of-thorns starfish – a notorious coral predator.

Then there are those animals that pierce and suck. Some parasitic worms and crustaceans suck the blood of fishes, and snails such as wentletraps and pyramidellids suck the body fluids of anemones and echinoderms.

The crown-of-thorns starfish, *Acanthaster planci*, everts its stomach over its prey, usually a coral colony, and, secreting digestive juices, kills it. The digested soup of tissues is then passed back on ciliary rows into the body to the voluminous caeca where nutrients are absorbed.

Finally there are the scavengers and detritovores — snails and worms, crabs, shrimps and other crustaceans, not to mention fishes — that will clean up dead bodies. There are beasts that specialize in coprophagy — eating faecal pellets — and those that shovel up sand and digest the life contained in it, for it is in the sands and sediments that most microbes live. These organisms complete the process of decomposition of organic matter to its chemical components so the cycle of nutrients can begin again.

All feeding methods are of significance in the economy of the Reef, but none are as fascinating as those of symbionts.

THE CROWN-OF-THORNS STARFISH

The 1980s have seen a resurgence of debate about the crown-of-thorns starfish, *Acanthaster planci*, and its effect on the Great Barrier Reef. Controversy began over 20 years ago when the first outbreaks occurred on the Reef. There were few people then, either within or outside scientific circles, who were prepared to state that the starfish could do serious damage. Today we know more, but are little closer to understanding the nature of the starfish's impact on the Reef.

The crown-of-thorns feeds primarily on staghorn corals (*Acropora*), the Reef's dominant hard corals. With the aid of hundreds of small suckers (tube feet) starfish climb onto a coral colony and then push out or evert their voluminous stomach over the colony. Digestive juices pour out and the tissues of the coral polyps are liquified and drawn back into the starfish. During digestion the starfish releases chemicals which attract others to the feeding site. The more starfish on one site the more chemicals released and hence an even greater number of starfish converge.

The starfish eats with remarkable efficiency, but does not devour every polyp. Polyps at the tip of the staghorn may survive, and it is these that will spawn, resulting in regrowth. The Acroporid corals grow quickly, and it has been suggested that outbreaks of the crown-of-thorns starfish may contribute to the rich species diversity of the Reef by consuming the fast-growing corals. This would allow the slow-growing corals a greater chance to propagate.

Others argue that population explosions have increased since the Reef has seen much more human activity, that the number of natural predators has declined and, as a consequence, the starfish outbreaks are worse.

Mostly scientists have been reluctant to make assertions about *Acanthaster planci*, believing there are no simple answers to the complex biological and geological questions surrounding the issue. Within the scientific community some say that immediate action should be taken, but others believe, with the present state of knowledge, quick action could be ill-advised. More research is certainly needed.

Staghorn coral *(Acropora)* overwhelmed by marauding crown-of-thorns starfish. Feeding starfish release chemicals which attract others to the group. The coral skeleton will be quickly overgrown with algae when the swarm moves on.

An encounter. The crown-of-thorns starfish leaves the plate coral revealing a bleached feeding scar from which all the living tissue has been removed.

A pair of cleaner wrasses, *Labroides dimidiatus*, at work. Cleaners drum on the surface of fish to quieten them and a pair will move over the surface feeding on mucus.

A young cleaner? Or is this a blenny mimic? The striking linear blue and black pattern signals that this fish is a cleaner.

SYMBIOSIS is living together. As in a crowded city the pressure to share a place to live or food is great. Some benefit from this, some exploit it.

Symbolic of life on the Reef is the relationship between small wrasses and larger fishes — cleaning symbiosis. On every reef some promontory or bommie that is readily recognizable will be the focus of life for a small group of fish, *Labroides*. All the fish of the group will clean, but in each group there is a dominant pair that undertake most of the cleaning. The fish are about 10-12 cm long, have a dark stripe from nose to tail and have a dark dorsal fin. Their swimming is jerky and they do not venture far from their territory.

The cleaners feed on mucus on the skin of other fishes, but also will eat any interesting items there — a parasitic copepod or worm, some fungus or bacterial soup about a wound or even a little flap of flesh. Surprisingly they are not only tolerated by other fishes, but are actively sought out.

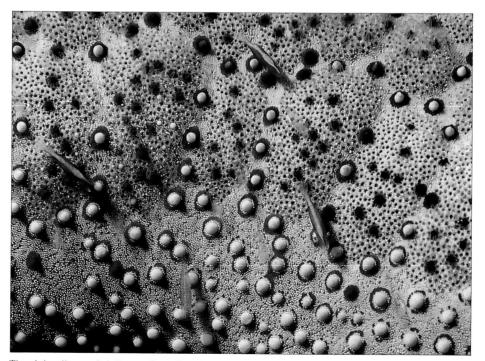

Tiny shrimp live out their lives on the surface of a starfish.

A giant clam with a spectacular mantle pattern. These colours are in part due to fields of enclosed zooxanthellae which help the clam to build its massive calcium shells.

Cleaners have preferred clients which they will pursue more dedicatedly than others. To avoid misunderstandings, especially with a big predator such as a coral trout, the cleaner will approach with an exaggeration of its jerky swimming. This 'dance', during which the dark dorsal fin and tail are extended at each short advance, serves to signal the fish's good intentions. Once it has recognized the cleaner, the client fish will adopt a passive position and wait for attention.

Many fishes will solicit the attention of the wrasses by invoking invitation displays. Parrotfish, for example, hang head up in the water and seem to ogle the cleaner. Often working as a pair, the dominant male and female can quickly induce a trance-like state in each of the big fish waiting to be cleaned. They do this by drumming on the fish's skin with their pelvic fins. Each fish may remain quiescent for up to a minute; a queue forms and a busy pair of cleaners can process more than 200 clients an hour.

Cleaners approach and clean different fishes in different ways, and the client fishes invite attention in different ways. Complicating matters even more, all manner of fishes, usually as juveniles, will clean others. Many shrimps are cleaners too. We have much to learn about this fascinating behaviour and its significance within reef ecosystems.

The sabre-toothed blenny, *Aspidinotus* is about the size of a cleaner, coloured and patterned like a cleaner and even able to swim like a cleaner. It is known as the cleaner mimic. It does not clean, however, but will 'fool' a young or inexperienced fish and then will bite out a chunk of flesh!

Another symbol of coral reefs is the clownfish nestled in the stinging folds of an anemone. Clownfish are mainly of the genus *Amphiprion*, closely related to damselfish. The anemones they favour are the giants of the family *Stoichactidae* which can grow to nearly one metre across. It has been suggested that the bright little clowns lure predators into the lethal grasp of the anemone. This is not true.

A parrotfish assumes an inviting posture while being cleaned by the cleaner wrasse.

A clownfish nestles in the stinging tentacles of its host and its home. The mucus on its surface protects it from harm.

A banded shrimp, *Stenopus*, is a cleaner which waits under a ledge moving its white antennae in a shaft of sunlight to attract custom.

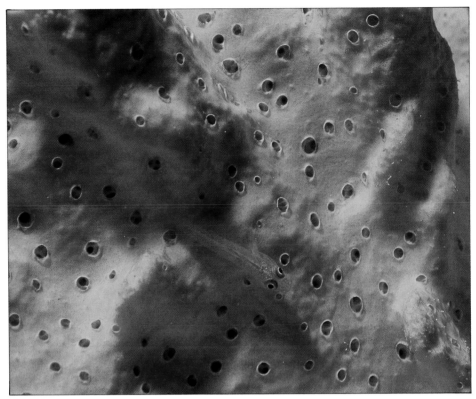

A tiny fish blends with its background, the sponge, which protects it from predators.

The anemones feed mainly by catching falling or drifting food and they have batteries of stinging cells along their tentacles for this purpose. The tentacles do not sting each other for the mucus covering them effectively inhibits the triggering of the nematocysts. Clownfish are weak swimmers and like their damselfish relatives set up small territories. They will dart back into shelter if necessary, but will defend their territory, their anemone, from potential predators such as some butterfly fish.

The clowns shelter in the anemones and to do this they acquire a mucus coat that protects them from the stings of their host. The nature of this cloak of mucus is still not understood. Some evidence suggests it is merely collected from the anemone (i.e. a borrowed cloak of mucus). Juveniles and also those clowns that have lived with an inert and artificial anemone made from rubber bands seem to be protected. It may be that the clowns can induce a change to their own mucus coats.

The clowns gain much from the relationship — certainly shelter. As plankton feeders the clowns spend much of their time hovering above the anemone feeding, but, like most reef creatures, they are opportunistic and will feed on tasty morsels captured by the anemone. Should this food be too big they will feed it to the anemone. This symbiosis provides mutual benefits.

Other fishes live with corals. Damselfish — relatives of the clowns — shelter among the branches. On reef flats, close inspection of small, pink colonies of the coral *Pocillopora* may reveal one or two small species of goby — their pelvic fins

Sea spiders, *Pycnogonida*, are little known creatures. Here one is living with a soft coral.

modified to help cling to the coral — and some crabs. Crabs and fish share this space between the branches of the coral; here they keep tiny territories maintaining continual contact with wave of fin and tap of antenna.

Gobies also share spaces with other animals. In the sands about the reefs small shrimps, almost blind, dig tunnels in the shifting substrate for their home. Gobies take advantage of the efforts of the shrimps and move into their shelters. The gobies have good eyesight and, perching high on their fins outside the hole, they maintain continual contact with the shrimps. This contact between fish's fin and shrimp's antenna ensures a quick and safe retreat is possible for both.

Fishes shelter in sponges too, but perhaps the most fascinating home is the inside of a sea cucumber. The pearlfish, *Carapus*, is 10-12 cm long and rapier thin towards its tail. These fish hunt for plankton at night and on return to the sea cucumber they will nudge the anus with their nose. Since the sea cucumber breathes by drawing in water through its anus to irrigate the respiratory trees, the anus will eventually open. With lightning speed the pearlfish curls its body and inserts its tail into the anus. It wriggles backwards flexing its body left and right to open up the passage until finally its head disappears.

Sea cucumbers are hosts to a wide variety of creatures. Outside are found copepods and scale worms colour coded to match their background. The scale worms are territorial and repel others of their kind from living on their host. Inside the cloaca

A brittle star takes advantage of its association with a sea fan to trap passing food.

A spindle cowry living with its sea fan host. Here the mantle covers the shell and mimics its background.

small swimming crabs can be found and bivalves with greatly reduced shells. Lying within the body cavity, but attached to the gut, and so connected to the outside, are snails so modified that they resemble flaccid tubes filled with embryos. Only these, the veliger larvae, hint of the molluscan identity of these highly specialized parasites.

Many crustaceans and molluscs adopt a symbiotic life style. Corals, for example, are found with polychaete worms, barnacles, hermit crabs, bivalves and snails all burrowed into the skeleton. By and large these animals use the hard coral skeleton as a protective home while feeding on plankton by trapping it from the water or by sucking water in for filtering. Corals also have a rich and diverse fauna of shrimps that live with them.

One intriguing little reef character is the gall crab, *Hapalocarcinus*. The female settles on a growing tip of coral and irritates it so that it grows around and entombs her. She feeds by drawing in food from the passing water through small pores left in the coral. She remains imprisoned there, but safe from predation. The male is tiny and so can slip in and out of her coral cage to mate.

A tiny shrimp clambers among the stinging tentacles of its host anemone.

SEA ANEMONES AND SYMBIONTS

Sea anemones are flower-like animals closely related to corals, but lacking any skeleton. They are solitary and either burrow into sediments or attach themselves to rocks with an adhesive disc. Their simple body resembles a bucket rimmed with tentacles, each of which is covered with clusters of stinging cells, the cnidocysts. Anemones feed by stinging and engulfing their prey with their mobile tentacles.

Sea anemones lie scattered among the corals and rubble of the reef flat, tucked into crevices on the slope or largely buried in the sands of the lagoon. Rarely is the body revealed, just the tentacles of every hue cascading gently in the current or sinuously pumping and probing, alert to any touch that might mean food.

One of the great joys on the Reef is to probe gently and carefully among stinging tentacles to discover hidden there some symbiote — a crab or shrimp, or even a fish.

Somehow the sight of clown fish darting among the tentacles of some giant sea anemone evokes within us a special feeling of awe. These brilliant orange and white striped fishes (*Amphiprion*), of which there are several species, seem alternately cheeky or coy, pugnacious or shy. They are such common aquarium inhabitants, and so compulsively photogenic that they are instantly recognised.

These creatures were first reported together by the naturalist Collingwood over 100 years ago in the South China Sea. The association is complex involving subtle chemical and visual cues and is certainly not identical for each species pair.

Some clowns are quite host specific, *Amphiprion melanopus* for example, seems to live only with the anemone *Physobrachia*; others such as *A. clarkii* are hardier and more general in their choice of hosts. Sometimes a large anemone can have two or more pairs inhabiting its tentacles and will attack an invader in protection of their territory. One of the more aggressive species is *A. biaculeatus*.

Clown fish will dart out and feed on plankton, but are known to share a meal with their anemone. They also suck or nibble on the tips of tentacles. Perhaps they are feeding upon mucus, a food source of great importance on the Reef and one many symbiotes of corals and anemones favour. Mucus also seems to be the key to the fishes' protection among the fields of stinging tentacles.

When experimentally held apart from their hosts, fish lose their protection to some degree. These fish when reintroduced to an anemone, like juvenile fish, will favour the areas around the base of the anemone and away from the tentacles. Here they can become covered with mucus without the risk of being stung.

Clowns are not the only symbiotes found with anemones. A great variety of shrimps and crabs, e.g. *Noepetrolisthes oshimai,* as well as smaller creatures also find homes among the tentacles or around the base. Many of these animals cannot secrete their own mucus so must rely on that of the anemone. They use it for protection and for food. How clown fishes interact with these other symbiotes is not known.

Amphiprion melanopus

Amphiprion clarkii

Amphiprion biaculeatus

Amphiprion perideraion

Amphiprion clarkii

Neopetrolisthes oshimai

An enormous number of parasites live in or on reef animals. Among these the parasitic worms have complex life-cycles which can involve many different stages in a variety of hosts. The complex food webs on the reefs provide pathways for the parasites to reach their final host in which they mature. Because most of these creatures are inside others we have hardly begun to explore their world.

Recent work on zooxanthellae, once thought to be all one species of algae, suggests that many species or at least many strains exist. Corals with zooxanthellae are able to grow 2-3 times faster in sunlight than in the dark and nearly all the carbon fixed goes to the host. It is this relationship which, according to Dr John Veron of AIMS, 'is at the essence of the very existence of reefs'.

The Great Barrier Reef has so many known associations and so many more still to be discovered. We are at the stage of recognizing that associations exist; some appear casual, some obligatory, some co-operative, some exploitative. Until we understand a little more of how most of these associations function and why, the term symbiosis says it all. If success can be measured by numbers, symbioses are very successful indeed.

Crawling across the surface of its sea cucumber host, a tiny scale worm affects a colour pattern to disguise its presence.

The starfish, *Echinaster luzonicus,* has lost part of an arm. Starfish are able to regenerate lost limbs as the tiny bud of tissue on its arm shows.

REPRODUCTION of their own kind is *the* criterion of success for all living things, and there are many ways that this is done.

A starfish crushed by a falling rock may regenerate itself from a severed arm. A coral fragmented by a frightened turtle may grow, provided the pieces lodge suitably, into several new colonies (i.e. each one a clone, genetically identical with the parent). In each case cells or polyps reproduce themselves asexually by simply dividing.

A staghorn coral with strong axial polyps.

The formation of colonies is a special form of asexual reproduction and one common among the sessile animals of the Great Barrier Reef — especially the corals, the bryozoans (lace corals) and the ascidians. In this process one or more individuals are formed and pull away but do not separate from the parent body.

In the coral *Acropora* the axial polyp on each branch keeps budding off new individuals. Such branches can grow in excess of 15cm a year. In some corals a stolon grows out, like a runner on a strawberry plant, and a subsidiary colony or collection of individuals develops. In some ascidians the budding process is accompanied by the binary fission of whole colonies.

A soft coral colony buds new ones vegetatively.

The polyclad flatworm, *Pseudocerus flavomarginatus*, is typically hermaphroditic. Generally the male systems mature before the female, but both are then functional.

The way in which new individuals bud from the parent or environment they share determines the final pattern or appearance of the whole colony — whether it becomes encrusting, massive, branching or forms plates.

In the corals each individual within a colony is generally much like any other. In the related siphonophores (such as the Portuguese Man-o'-War or bluebottle) individual polyps may grow into quite different shapes with very different roles. One polyp may become a gas-filled float which keeps the colony at the surface, below are polyps specialized for stinging and feeding and others for breeding sexually.

Sexual reproduction is the most commonly practised reproductive mode, even among the lowly sponges and corals. These sessile organisms simultaneously release eggs and sperm for fertilization externally. Many fishes also do this, but in them and other more highly evolved animals sexual reproduction is the only way new individuals can be created.

Sex creates new combinations with every fertilized egg. These may be just sufficiently different to survive minor change or perhaps thrive in new conditions. Sex is innovative.

Separate males and females are not necessary for sexual reproduction. The phenomenon of hermaphroditism, being both male and female, is common on the Reef. In most corals the polyps produce both eggs and sperm at the same time (i.e. they are simultaneously male and female).

Most hermaphrodites are predominantly one sex at a time; in flatworms they may change slowly so that both systems operate simultaneously, or they may change rapidly, switching in a matter of hours as occurs in some fish. Time differences prevent self fertilization.

The spoonworm *Pseudobonellia* has males and females, but the sex is determined by where the planktonic larvae settle. Should one settle where no other worm lives nearby it will grow into a female; however, if one settles near a female it will enter the female and remain little more than a bundle of cells producing sperm. It becomes a parasitic male living inside the female.

In the peculiarly specialized and parasitic barnacles *Sacculina*, the first larva to settle out from the plankton burrows into a crab. It grows by sending rootlets throughout the crab until, like a mushroom, a sac containing ovaries and small empty receptacles finally pops out of the crab's abdomen. Subsequent larvae attach to the emergent sac and burrow through to the receptacles where they become merely bags of testes. The sac is then really two generations — one male, one female.

Fishes too have fascinating sex lives. Many fishes are, as we would expect, separate males and females and remain so all their lives. On the reef, however, some of the most conspicuous fishes change sex. In both the parrotfish and the wrasses, the juveniles settle out of the plankton as females — only females and always females.

Young parrotfish females tend to be drab. They will breed in this condition with similarly drab or slightly coloured males in a group spawning. At dusk, just after a full tide when currents flowing off the reef are strong, males and females will swim agitatedly near the reef crest. First one pair and then others will suddenly break away and dash for the surface, release eggs and sperm and then return to the bottom. Fertilized eggs are carried off the reef into the plankton.

A nudibranch laying its ribbon of eggs. These will hatch and a planktonic stage will follow.

A baby box fish. Juveniles often assume cryptic colour to avoid predation.

A pair of clowns. These fish may establish permanent pairs. Beginning life as males, they may change to female when no longer dominated and accept a new young male as a mate.

A pipefish rests in some coral. Both pipefish and sea horse males carry and brood the eggs.

Some females as they get older begin to change to males, and as they grow their colours increase in splendour. These older fish hold breeding territories into which they entice females for that quick upwards rush to spawn. So different are the colours of males and females that for a long time many were considered different species.

Brilliant colours among reef fishes are thought to be primarily sexual flags. In such a crowded environment with so many similar species, recognition of a partner of the same species is of paramount importance if sexual effort is not to be squandered.

The cleaner wrasse, *Labroides dimidiatus,* maintains small harems. Each juvenile female on gaining entry to the harem of 6-10 individuals begins a social battle for dominance. Eventually she may become the dominant female and thereby gains the opportunity to spawn with the single dominant male. Should the male disappear, within hours the dominant female begins to change to become the dominant male. In a little over a day the change has become irreversible.

Similar dominance groups are found in some clownfish, *Amphiprion.* Here, however, the fish begin life as males and the dominant fish of the group is a female — a reversal of roles. Some clowns are known to establish permanent pair bonds.

Whereas parrotfish and wrasses release their eggs into the plankton, clowns clean a little patch of rock near the base of their host anemone where they lay clusters of eggs. These are ferociously protected by the dominant male. Nest building and protection of eggs is also a characteristic of the related damselfish which are so common on the reefs.

Cardinal fish protect their young by carrying them about in their mouths, but the ultimate in protection of eggs comes with the pipefish and seahorses which cement their eggs to the male's body, even inside a pouch of skin in seahorses. The male broods the eggs, carrying them about until they finally hatch.

PROTECTION in this seemingly idyllic world of colour and form populated by a great diversity of life is important. It can be a tough place in which to live — tough to find and hold some space, food to eat and time to reproduce; a tough place too in which to avoid being attacked or eaten.

In its simplest form predator avoidance is merely choosing to live in a protected place. Small mobile creatures such as crabs, snails, brittlestars and worms seek out shelter, holes and crevices under, between and within the jumble of rocks and corals. Sedentary organisms also may survive if they settle in such places. Below each boulder or long-dead and upturned plate of coral lives a wealth of creatures.

Seeking shelter or protection is effective too if the shelter is alive. There are numerous associations — clownfish with anemones, fishes and crustaceans with corals, gobies and shrimps in burrows, crabs in turtle grass, pilot fish and sharks.

Hiding while being exposed is one way to survive. Some animals make themselves difficult to detect, most often by visually disrupting their outline with colours and

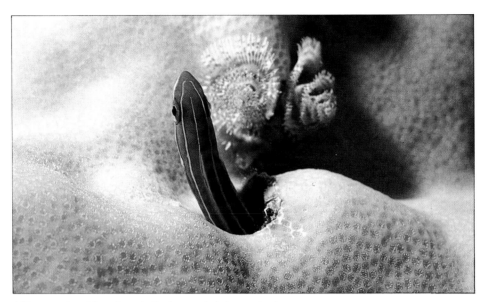

A blenny peeks out from its protective home, a hole in a coral colony.

patterns. Open water fish such as mackerel and sprats are dark above and pale below. This counter shading evens out the light reflecting from them so that they become much less easy to see, especially if they are still.

Remaining still and matching the background is the commonest form of camouflage and examples are found in nearly all the mobile groups — worms, molluscs, crustaceans, fishes. As if colour and form were not enough, to make the illusion complete some shrimps and pipefish rock gently to match their movements to that of their weedy background.

When removed from their reef environment animals such as the nudibranchs and some of the more exotically patterned fishes reveal striking colours. In their natural surroundings, however, among ascidians, sponges, algae and the numerous brightly-hued organisms of the Reef, these animals may be consummately camouflaged.

Camouflage is a protective device used by the cepholopods. Disruptive colouration is fast changing and accurate.

This sole normally lives in a hollow below a shallow boulder. Disturbed, his cover is blown.

The master of sedentary disguise is the stonefish. Here beauty of colour and form can hardly be claimed unless perfection is beauty enough. Even isolated in an aquarium these moderately large fish, 25cm long, can be very hard to detect.

Other animals can change colour rapidly by expanding and contracting starshaped cells in their skin that are full of pigments. These animals are able to recreate the colours of the background upon which they settle. Flatfishes are good at this, but unquestionably for speed and accuracy the octopus is supreme. It can move, stop and disappear before the eyes. After years spent diving on the Reef, Dr Gerry Goeden of Queensland Fisheries estimates he has 'spent several hours aware only of a small octopus or cuttlefish going through its rainbow of colour and shape changes as it swims across the bottom. They seem to operate by the rules — if you can see it, then copy it.'

Almost disappearing against the background, the trumpet fish stares warily at the camera.

For some animals physical appearance is not as important for protection as their behaviour. Scallops, their mantle rimmed with tiny eyes, can detect a shadow. By rapidly clapping together their valves they can swim quickly and erratically away. Prawns and crayfish can snap their abdomen up towards their body with powerful muscles. This jerks the body rapidly backwards. Squid and cuttlefish depart similarly

There is protection in numbers in this school of goatfish.

by using jet propulsion. They contract their muscular body about a column of water and this causes them to shoot away. If sufficiently disturbed they may also pour out a cloud of ink to mask their departure.

Most fishes swim rapidly and erratically to avoid a predator, sometimes even leaping from the water. Flying fish have perfected this and by spreading their pectoral fins and sculling with their tail they can reach speeds of 60km/h as they glide and skim across the surface of the waves. Schooling fishes have obvious advantages in open water in avoiding attack — the school looks big, each individual's movement protects it as just one in a confusing mass and there are many more eyes to see danger.

Slow moving creatures also need protection. The heavy shell of most molluscs serves this purpose, indeed it may be borrowed by a hermit crab. Turtles have armour too, though flippers are easy prey and are often seen with scalloped edges revealing an encounter with a predator.

An armoured carapace was not sufficient to protect this turtle. The flippers are vulnerable.

Sedentary polychaete worms build a tube for protection. These tubes may be muddy, parchment-like, may contain sand and shell, or ultimately may incorporate calcium and be very hard.

More active forms of defence can be seen in those animals which have spines or poisons. Echinoderms have hard plates in their skin. In the sea urchin *Diadema* these may be long, needle-like spines. Normally sea urchins are protected from tiny creatures wishing to settle between their spines by small jawed structures, the pedicellariae. These are armed with poison glands in the sea urchin *Toxopneustes*. The notorious crown-of-thorns starfish also has spines and these are covered with skin filled with poisonous glands.

Scorpaenid fishes, notably the lion fish *Pterois volitans*, and particularly the related stonefish have developed a combination of spine and glands which are effective in delivering a discouraging message. The spines of the stonefish lock upright and so penetrate when flesh is pressed down upon them. The pressure serves to stretch

123

the skin and to squeeze venom from the gland at the base of the spine upwards and deep into the wound. Stingrays also have venom glands associated with a spine near the base of the tail. These fish can quickly twist and thrust upwards to dissuade predators.

Spines alone can be quite effective. Polychaete worms such as *Chloeia* or *Eurythoe* have bundles of spines that can penetrate quickly and deeply. These are so exceedingly fine that they often cannot be seen, but continue to prickle and to irritate the skin for days. Porcupine fish are covered with spines and, coupled with a habit of pumping themselves up with water like the related toad and pufferfish, they can resemble spiny balls — most unpalatable. The surgeon fish has spurs on the base of its tail, one each side, directed forward and scalpel sharp. These elegant fish with their slim lines and crisp colours can lacerate predators or romantic rivals alike.

The colours of the butterfly cod serve warning. His spines are deadly.

Sticky cuvierian tubules spew forth from the cloaca of this sea cucumber to entangle and entrap an attacker.

Coral wars: outward growth here is thwarted by the aggressive stings of the competitor for space.

Poisons are sometimes borrowed. The planktonic nudibranchs *Glaucus* feed on siphonophores such as the Portuguese Man-o'-War. They are able to ingest the stinging cells of their prey without triggering them. These are then incorporated into the molluscs' skin for their own use. Other nudibranchs which feed on sponges can accumulate the chemical defences of their prey into their own bodies. These highly toxic materials provide defence for the molluscs.

A protective device found in nearly all the creatures of the Great Barrier Reef is mucus. Clownfish use this most effectively. In flat worms, ribbon worms, corals, sponges, molluscs and fishes copious mucus stops organisms settling on and invading the skin. Many sponges incorporate antibacterial agents (i.e. antibiotics) which makes these animals of great interest to pharmaceutical companies.

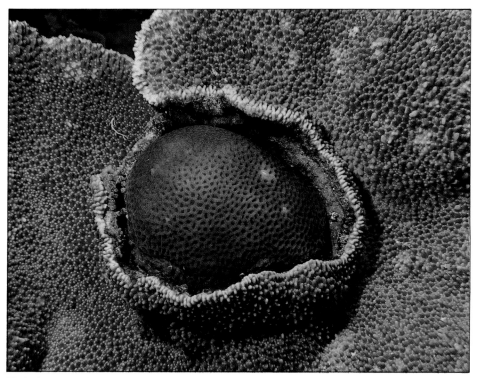

The brain coral has its personal space which cannot be invaded.

DUGONGS

The mermaid myth is believed to have originated with this strange creature. Reminiscent of a cow lumbering along the bottom of the sea grazing the sea grasses, it is perhaps difficult to imagine how the dugong resembles the legendary mermaid who lured sailors and their ships into dangerous waters. A shyer, less malicious creature than the dugong would be hard to find.

Its appearance, at first glance, is similar to that of a dolphin, but it is slower moving and less streamlined. The dugong's head is heavy and blunt, with the mouth on the underside of the head, convenient for grazing. The few coarse hairs around its mouth serve as sensors, searching out the best grasses as it moves along.

The dugong is one of the few surviving sirenians, or sea cows. Other members of the sirenian family became extinct through man's activities in the last century. The closest surviving relatives of the dugong today are the manatees, found in areas of the Caribbean, the Amazon and West Africa, but these are freshwater mammals. The dugong is the only one of the family to be found in marine water and is entirely herbivorous, living off the seaweeds found on the floor of shallow seas.

Dugongs were probably fairly common at one time, but have disappeared from many areas over the years. It is believed that one of the largest surviving populations of dugongs in the world now resides in the waters of the Great Barrier Reef. The Reef is, therefore, an important area of conservation for this rarely observed creature. Aerial watches monitor the herds' population and movement: divers are lucky to see a dugong at all in Reef waters, justifying its reputation of being shy and retiring. It is the lush sea grass of some areas of the Reef and the warm shallow waters for breeding which make it an ideal habitat for these animals.

Dugongs move in herds of up to several hundred. Although they have a life span of around 70 years they are a slow breeding animal, and so their population is closely watched by Marine Park researchers. Females do not calve until they are at least ten years old and they produce a single calf every three to seven years, usually between September and January. There is a strong bond between mother and calf; the calves suckle for up to 18 months, and stay with their mothers for two years.

Dugong meat is considered a great delicacy and hunting dugongs is an important part of Aboriginal culture. The Government has allowed the traditional hunting for dugongs to continue but hunting licences are only issued to Aboriginal hunters who live on the Reserves.

Nevertheless a close watch is maintained by researchers to ensure the dugong population is not adversely affected by hunting. So far the practice is not thought to be endangering the numbers, but the animals face other hazards such as fishing nets and the shark nets that protect swimmers. Positive action may be required in the future to protect these gentle creatures of the sea.

A young dugong tags along with its mother. The bond is strong and young will stay with their mothers for two years.

A scarred and battered snout precedes this dugong as it glides over its feeding grounds.

Truly like a sea cow, the dugong feeds in the seagrass meadows.

127

Parrotfish use mucus in a novel way. At night these fish often sleep in a coral crevice, but wrapped in a cloak or cocoon of mucus that effectively seals in their smells and masks them from marauding nocturnal predators such as eels.

A peculiar defence found in some sea cucumbers is the habit of pouring out copious, long and very sticky threads, called cuvierian tubules, which entangle and immobilize predators. Corals may use long threads lined with nematocysts extruded from their gut to attack others which invade or grow in their space. Some soft corals can use chemical 'fences' to create a 5-10cm zone free of crowding about them.

When we explore the Great Barrier Reef we also need to protect ourselves. The most widespread stings come from the coelenterates — hydroids, firecoral, corals, anemones, siphonophores and jellyfishes.

Finally we also must protect ourselves from toxic or dangerous substances we may eat. Ciguatera is a form of food poisoning associated with eating certain fishes, especially mackerel. Its symptoms include numbness, tingling and pains in muscles and joints. Although some evidence suggests it may be associated with physical disturbance of the reefs or algal blooms, there does not appear to be any pattern or predictability to outbreaks.

Barracuda. Speed, strength and ferocious teeth mean these top predators have few enemies.

RHYTHMS, predictable and regular, dominate life on the Reef. As the sun rises on each new day the daily cycle of light and dark begins anew. Little light penetrates the water at first as the angle of the sun is so low, but as the sun rises it soon illuminates the surface waters bringing colour and energy.

The sun wields other powers. Its mighty gravitational pull ensures the earth traces on orbit about it with the tilt of the earth's axis determining the seasons. Furthermore, the pull of the earth keeps the moon in thrall. As the earth spins on its axis the waters of the oceans roll across its surface. They are subject to the centrifugal force of the planet's spin and the competing gravitational pulls of sun and moon. The result is the tides.

The green turtle, if it survives its first 50 years, may return to its island of birth to lay its eggs, starting the long cycle of life anew.

Each day two watery bulges are driven over and around the earth's surface and each month the moon adds or subtracts its gravitational pull to that of the sun producing large tides (springs) at new moon and small tides (neaps) at full moon.

The sun heating the surface waters causes water, not salts, to evaporate from the surface and rise into the air, condensing as clouds in the cooler, upper atmosphere. The heat of the sun also causes the air above and the water below to rise: currents of convection are born and, empowered by the sun, winds and waves move across the surface of the sea.

Winds, waves, currents and tides combine with the daily, lunar and seasonal rhythms to dictate the lives of organisms on the Reef.

As the sun rises on the Reef, photosynthesis begins. The corals fold away their tentacles and allow the sun to reach their zooxanthellae: the creatures of the night fade away into dim crevices to wait again for darkness. Parrotfish break out of their cocoons, wrasses and cods emerge from their hiding places and the daily round begins.

Terns stream home at the end of the day.

For reefs which do not break the surface at low tide, the tidal influence is still felt. 'Everything,' says Dr Gerry Goeden, 'is constantly being swept along or pulled at by tidal currents. It brings animals their food and conveys away their offspring. It sand-blasts creatures attached to the bottom and creates havoc with burrowing animals. It brings life, it destroys, it moves, it re-shapes the entire underwater world every six hours.'

Where coral heads break the surface or sands of a cay are exposed another habitat is created — the intertidal. Epitomized by a reef heron stalking its prey across an exposed reef flat, this habitat is the most vulnerable to the interplay of the natural rhythms. Organisms here must adjust to periodic exposure to sun and air or even to torrents of fresh water from tropic storms. Here too are the added dangers of the terrestrial predators such as the heron.

Because the moon's period is 29.5 days, tides are not at a regular daily time, but occur nearly an hour later each day. Exposure in the intertidal can be as harsh as noon in mid-summer or as gentle as a dawn in spring. Water temperatures can get high, exceeding $30°C$, causing great stress. Corals may pour out mucus that forms rope-like threads across the reef flat; bubbles of gas can lift algal mats in tide pools along the beach rock. To conserve moisture snails cluster together forming little heaps. Even when the snails are held in aquaria with a constant depth of water these clusters will form at the time of each low tide.

There seems to be no pattern to past recorded climate in tropical Queensland. Biologists at AIMS and elsewhere are hoping, however, to interpret the banding patterns contained in the skeletons of large corals such as *Porites*. They are seeking a correlation with climatic events which, like tree rings, may reveal a history stretching back several hundred years.

There is growing evidence from sedimentary data that the Crown-of-Thorns starfish have occurred previously in plague proportions at intervals of about 400 years. We are a long way, however, from understanding such phenomena.

The rhythms we know and those we can only guess at control or at least influence marine life on the Great Barrier Reef. The seasonal gathering of turtles or humpback whales to breed, the lunar rhythms and daily rhythms of tides and light all interplay to govern feeding, spawning and dispersal of reef creatures. The rise and fall of plankton, the opening and closing of the polyps, the clustering of the snails, the foraging of herons — all these hinge on the turning of the celestial bodies.

So next time you see the full moon of early summer begin to wane, think of the Great Barrier Reef. There mutton birds will be crashing in to find their nesting hole, to sit and socialize all night, female turtles will be hauling up the beach to dig a hole and to lay their eggs, and down below the water's surface the corals will be spawning.

Forty tonnes of humpback somersaults backwards out of the water.

WHALES

Before the days of commercial whaling, humpback whales were a common sight in Reef waters. A few years ago they were close to extinction but today, as a protected species, the population is slowly recovering and it is estimated that there are about 1200 in the vicinity of the Great Barrier Reef. A glimpse of a whale, the largest and perhaps most spectacular of all living creatures, is still a relatively rare and exciting occasion.

It has proved difficult to study whales and to keep track of their movements, but it is thought that those which are seen in the Reef waters breed there, attracted by the warm shallow waters. They migrate to the Antarctic for summer, and return each year to Australian waters in July, staying there till October.

Whales are actually mammals, belonging to the same order (Cetacea) as porpoises and dolphins. The cetaceans have evolved from land-based animals into stream-lined swimming animals able to live their entire life in the water. They are warm-blooded mammals, that need air to breathe and that suckle their young as do terrestial animals, and their more animal-like physical features have adapted to life in the water. For instance, instead of nostrils whales breathe through the blowhole on the top of their heads and the forelimbs have developed into strong swimming flippers.

There are two main types of whales: the whalebone or baleen whales (*Mysticeti*) and the toothed whales (*Odontoceti*). They are distinguished by their feeding mechanisms. The whalebone whales draw huge quantities of sea water into their mouths and then 'strain' it out again through the hundreds of whalebone plates (baleen) which are attached to the upper jaw, leaving krill (small crustacea) trapped in the baleen. They then eat what is cleaned off the baleen by the tongue. The toothed whales, in contrast, actively hunt down fish and squid and swallow them whole.

This humpback reveals a lower jaw encrusted with barnacles. The barnacles also feed on plankton.

Graceful flukes stream with water.

Several species of whale are known to frequent the Great Barrier Reef waters. Those most frequently observed, because of their surfacing and diving activities, are the humpback whales. Members of the whalebone family, humpbacks can grow up to 15 metres in length and weigh up to 40 tonnes. The humpback derives its name from the way in which it appears to hump its back when preparing to dive after surfacing. Another distinguishing feature of this whale is the way in which it presents its distinctive tail fluke above the surface of the water. Research scientists are using photographs of sighted tail flukes to identify individual whales, as the markings and scars distinguish one whale from another.

Other members of the whalebone family have been reported in the area, including minke and blue whales, but these are very rare sightings. Blue whales are the largest species, growing to 31 metres and weighing up to 160 tonnes.

Whalebone whales are also distinct from the toothed whales in that they are usually seen alone or in small groups, called pods, whereas the more sociable toothed whales nearly always move in larger groups. Species of toothed whales include sperm whales, killer whales and pilot whales. Sperm whales, however, prefer deep water and so are unlikely to be seen near the Reef.

For the present the scarce population makes any whale sighting a rare moment. It is ironic that most of our limited knowledge of whales was gleaned from the dead carcasses of commercially harvested whales. Today they are protected and it is hoped that as the whale population increases, sightings of this spectacular inhabitant of the Reef will be more common and our knowledge of them more complete.

A navigational adjustment. A humpback wallows in calm seas.

WHERE NATURE IS ART

MARK GOYEN

OASES within deserts, cities more bizarre and colourful than any terrestrial environment — the Reef is all this and more. Words are inadequate to describe beauty of this order; there is a look of wonder on the faces of those who experience this world for the first time. Gliding over gardens and canyons of brilliant coral is breathtaking — but ponder a moment and reflect on this aquatic world. The Reef is composed of millions of tiny, beautiful and unique organisms which merge to form magnificent structures. Repetition, symmetry and variation are endemic to a coral reef. They are, respectively, the bases of life, the consequences of life and the fuel for survival through evolution. Photography, the key to comprehending these principles, allows each organism, each coral, each fish to be appreciated in all their colour and complexity. And, as their dramatic beauty is revealed, so life becomes art.

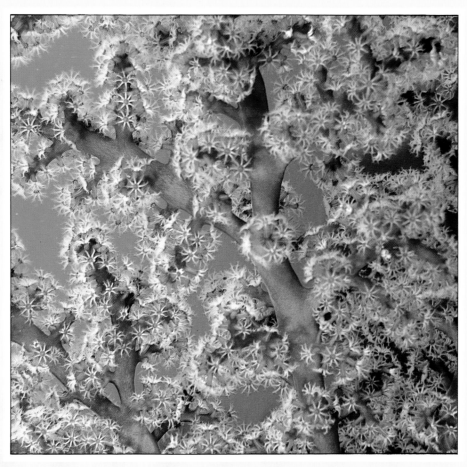

Soft coral polyps

Sea anemone, tentacle tips

Clam, *Tridacna maxima*, exhalant siphon

Tubastrea polyps

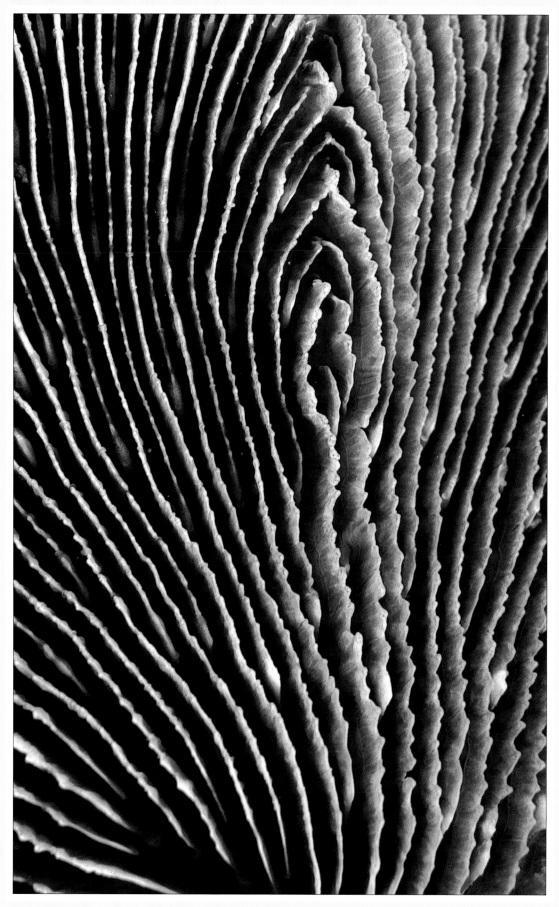

Mushroom coral

Feather star

Hard coral, *Physogyra*

Clam, *Tridacna maxima*, inhalant siphon

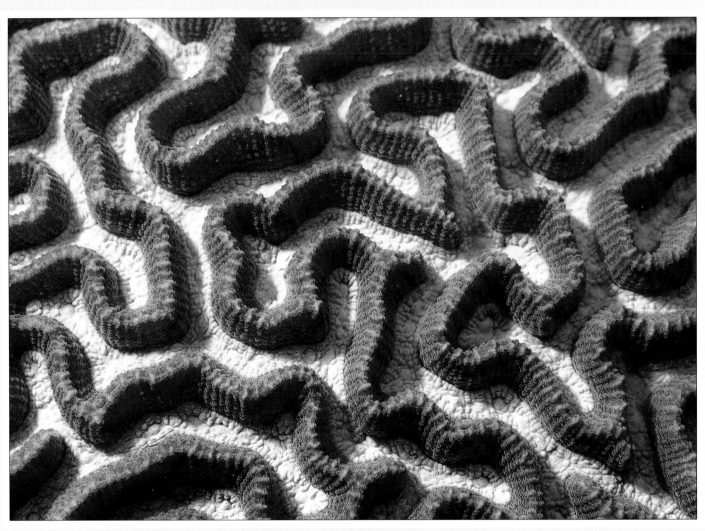

Brain coral

Feather star on sea fan

Whip coral and goby

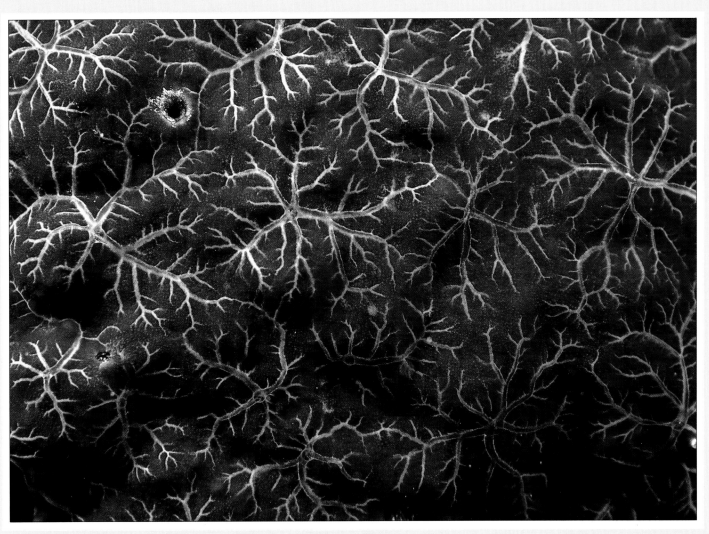

Encrusting sponge

Weedy scorpion fish *Rhinopias frondosa*

Goby on soft coral

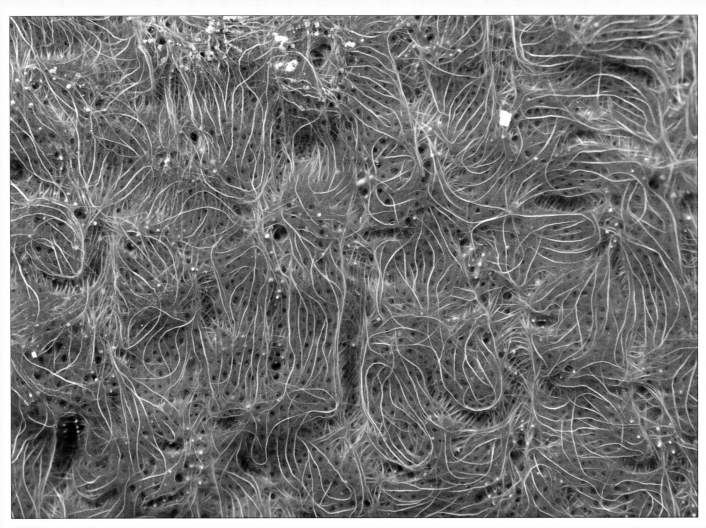

Encrusting sponge

Soft coral polyps, *Xenia elongata*

Hard coral, *Diploastrea heliopora*

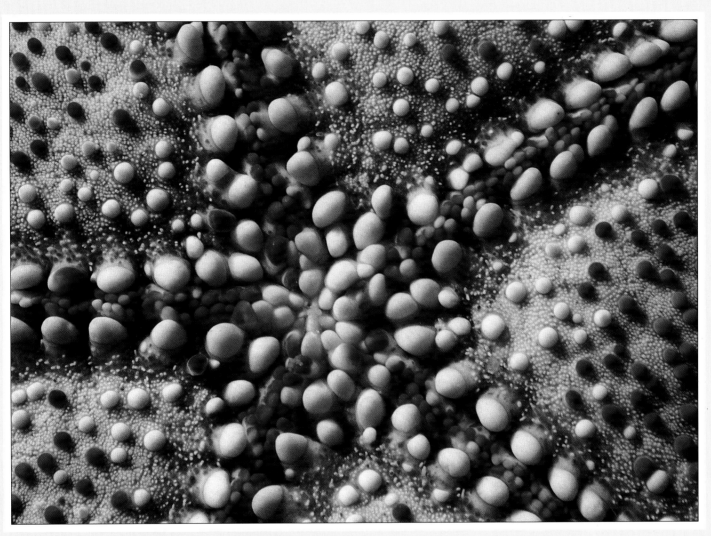

Pincushion starfish, *Culcita novaeguineae*, underside

THE LIFE ABOVE

HAROLD HEATWOLE

VIEWED from the air, the cays of the Great Barrier Reef appear as verdant emeralds set in golden sand. Mounted on a turquoise reef, edged with a filigree of sparkling foam, they lie above water, yet are as much a part of the Reef as the corals and fish. Seabirds and sea turtles obtain food from the ocean but require land for breeding. Ghost crabs almost seem like land animals as they scurry across the sand at low tide. At high tide they become part of an aquatic world. Some small cays are submerged sand bars at high tide but become emergent islands at low tide; thus they alternate between the land and sea environments several times each day. Are they frequently-submerged islands or occasionally-emergent sandbars? The answer to this question is a semantic one, depending on how one defines an island. But the question does draw attention to an important fact — that land and sea are intimately bound on the Great Barrier Reef and there is no sharp dividing line between marine and terrestrial environments.

This small emerald strip of vegetation on Frigate Cay contrasts sharply with the brilliant white beach and the deep surrounding waters.

DISTRIBUTION OF FLORA AND FAUNA

For plants to become established in new habitats they must have some effective way of spreading their seeds. This is a problem on mainlands as well as from mainlands to islands. The kinds of adaptations that disperse seeds are both numerous and amazing. Some have fluffy little parachutes and are wind-blown; others are carried by birds, either in the digestive tract or attached to the feathers; and still others float and are carried by water currents.

Strangely, wind dispersal is the least important method of transporting plants to islands. Many of the common plants on the cays of the Great Barrier Reef are sea-dispersed. The seeds are buoyant, either because of air-filled spaces or corky materials. They remain afloat for weeks or even months and may be carried thousands of kilometres to be cast up on some distant shore. Not all seeds that remain afloat for long periods live to reach a new habitat. Some species are intolerant to salt and soon die in sea water, their dead husks littering beaches around the world. Others are highly resistant to salt and may even require soaking in sea water before they are capable of germinating. Plant species with buoyant seeds differ greatly in their sensitivity to sea water — some can cross only short water gaps while others can survive a trip across a major ocean.

Animals have similar problems. Those that are strong fliers, such as birds, bats, butterflies, moths and dragonflies, are able to reach islands easily under their own power. On the other hand, many weak fliers or even small, flightless species can be wafted on air currents and blown long distances. Some baby spiders spin little silk parachutes, called gossamer, that catch the wind and take the animal aloft. Traps on aircraft high above mid-ocean have picked up a surprising variety of small organisms.

The prevailing wind on the Great Barrier Reef is from the south east, coming from the sea rather than the mainland. Consequently, most of the time winds are unfavourable for transporting animals. When the wind does swing around and comes from the mainland, large numbers of moths and butterflies, not usually present on the islands, sometimes appear.

A butterfly comes to rest in a cakile flower on Bell Cay, part of the Swain Reefs.

Animals also may be carried by sea currents, but usually raft on logs, coconuts or other debris. To many people such a means of getting around seems to stretch credulity. Even Thomas Barbour, a famous naturalist of the first part of this century, scoffed at it. Had he examined these miniature arks, as scientists did some decades later, he would have been amazed. Floating debris of terrestrial origin often contains a surprising variety of live animals. Spiders, snails, false-scorpions, mites, millipedes, slaters, worms and many species of insects from 19 different families have all been recovered live from flotsam. On larger pieces, such as entire trees washed out to sea, vertebrate animals including lizards, snakes, toads, mammals and even a crocodile have been found.

Driftwood, seen here on North East Cay in the Saumarez Reef, plays an important part in bringing new life to the cays.

It is true that animals do not arrive on an island every day by this means. Yet, it is not uncommon either. Many remote cays, either lacking vegetation altogether or with only low plants, have driftwood logs, or even nearly-complete dead trees, lying on their beaches. It is difficult to imagine how large ground-spiders or large centipedes reach distant islands other than by rafting.

Humans are very important in dispersing animals and plants to islands. Sometimes it is done intentionally. Those islands of the Great Barrier Reef, inhabited for a long time, or with resorts or lighthouses on them, have a variety of ornamental herbs, shrubs and trees that were obviously planted on purpose. In a few cases these plants have escaped from captivity and spread more widely on the island. Lady Elliot Island, practically denuded of vegetation by guano miners at the turn of the century, has been magnificently restored by plantations of she-oaks. Goats were intentionally introduced onto many small islands of the Great Barrier Reef as a food source for shipwrecked mariners. They caused severe damage to the vegetation and, although they were removed some years ago, not all of the islands have completely recovered from their effect.

Many plants and animals have been introduced unintentionally by humans. Weed species are more numerous on islands that have frequent traffic than on those visited less often. That may be a direct effect of people inadvertently carrying seeds on their clothing or in their belongings, but it may be partly an indirect effect. Humans, with their associated refuse and scraps, provide an easy living for gulls. Gulls eat weed seeds and carry live ones in their digestive tracts. These germinate after being cast out with the excrement. Thus, the high numbers of weeds on islands with a great volume of human traffic may be because humans attract gulls that disperse weed seeds, as well as people carrying seeds themselves.

Domestic cockroaches are common on inhabited islands. North West Island, in the Capricornia or southern section of the Reef, has a population of feral domestic cats and even a population of domestic fowl. The worst scourge of all, however, is the presence of rats. They prey on sea birds' eggs and young, and are an even greater ecological disaster on islands than they are on a mainland. Many are accidentally introduced by humans, but in some cases they probably swam ashore from ships wrecked on the Reef.

S U R V I V A L

Since green plants manufacture the food upon which all other life ultimately depends, it is a reasonable guess that they will be the first to be established on a newly-formed island. Then animals that eat plants (herbivores) might appear, followed by predators that eat herbivores, and so on. As logical as that sounds, it usually doesn't happen that way. The reason is that a young cay still depends for nourishment on the sea that gave it birth. It has not yet become 'weaned'. Dead fish and other marine creatures wash up on its beaches and the first land animals to become established are scavenging beetles and flies. Sea birds roosting or breeding on the island produce excrement (guano) that also serves as food for scavengers. Next to appear are predators on the scavengers, such as spiders and centipedes. Land plants often become established next, followed by the herbivores that eat them. Finally, predators that eat herbivores or feed on other predators become part of the fauna.

As an island becomes larger, and develops a dense cover of vegetation, it becomes increasingly independent of the sea. Food for its inhabitants is produced by the ever increasing cover of land plants and proportionately less is supplied directly from the ocean. This makes it possible for the establishment of still more species of herbivores and their predators. Eventually the scavenger industry will become small compared to that based directly on green land plants.

Not all animals and plants that successfully reach an island alive become established there. They must find a favourable habitat. Some plants do not germinate in the insular environment. Their seeds may lie dormant until they have exhausted their stored food and then die without ever sprouting. Others germinate but the seedlings invariably die at a young age because of the harsh conditions they encounter, never having reached maturity and set seed. Still others may grow and reproduce for a while and become temporarily established, but eventually die out under the rigours of insular life. Only a small proportion of the species of plants are permanent residents. A high species turnover is a characteristic of islands, especially small ones.

Similarly, solitary animals that immigrate fail to find a mate and, unless it is a female already with eggs, the species will die out with the death of the lone migrant. Species that do become established vary greatly in the length of time they last before becoming locally extinct. On One Tree Island, in the Capricornia section of the Reef, a total of 396 species of insects were recorded over a period of a little more than three years. Of these, over half were species that never became established as breeding populations. Most of the rest became established for a while, only to die out eventually. Just 26 species, or less than 7% of the total, were permanent residents. Truly, islands are dynamic places.

New life has arrived on Price Cay in the form of this sprouting seed.

In time the vegetation establishes itself as on this remote cay in the Swain Reefs.

DEVELOPMENT OF VEGETATION

PIONEER SPECIES

The first plants to appear on a cay are hardy species that are sea-dispersed, salt tolerant, drought-resistant and can grow on shifting sands that are poor in nutrients. These are the pioneer species.

Goat's-foot convolvulus, *Ipomoea pes-caprae*, subspecies *brasiliensis*, has buoyant, salt resistant seeds and is dispersed by sea currents. It rapidly colonises loose sand by sending out long, prostrate stems. These two characteristics make it a common pioneer plant on beaches. However, that habitat is one which is very unstable because of beach erosion and the effect of storms. Goat's-foot is sometimes washed out completely on small islands, to disappear temporarily until new seeds again wash up on the beach. It occurs around all the tropical oceans of the world.

Stalky grass, *Lepturus repens*, is widespread on the Great Barrier Reef, being found on many islands, even small, remote ones. It is rather ordinary in appearance, yet it is tenacious. In several ways it has the best of both worlds. It has two different growth forms. Sometimes it is prostrate with long stems creeping over the ground. At the joints new roots are formed that penetrate the sand. It can also grow as an upright bunch-grass. Sometimes the two forms grow side by side and it isn't certain just what causes the difference. The bunch-grass form frequently serves as a shelter for birds that nest in vegetation. This species also has two means of dispersing its seeds. The seeds are buoyant and can be carried by sea currents. In addition, they have small teeth on the edges that allow them to cling to feathers and thus be dispersed by birds.

Bird's-beak grass, *Thuarea involuta*, also grows by long creeping runners and has wide, light-green leaves that are very soft and velvety. It is difficult to see how something so soft can survive in such a harsh, sand-blasted environment. The fruits each contain two seeds surrounded by an enclosed air space that makes them buoyant and easily dispersed by sea. This species has an unusual inflorescence for a grass; its fancied resemblance to a bird's beak gave rise to its common name.

The sea rocket, *Cakile edentula*, is common only in the southern part of the Great Barrier Reef, but is likely to become established throughout a wider area. It also has a fascinating history. The sea rocket is not a native plant, but an American one that probably arrived in Australia in the ballasts of sailing ships sometime prior to 1863. It became established near Melbourne and spread north along the coastline,

Goat's foot convolvulus blooms on Bell Cay in the Swain Reefs.

Amazingly the delicate-looking bird's beak grass survives the harshest conditions.

first reaching the Barrier Reef in the 1950s. It inhabits the upper edges of beaches, primarily because it is salt resistant and can grow in soils that are too salty for many species of plants. It is unable to compete successfully with the more dense vegetation that grows further inland. Its fruit is in two parts, with the outer part drying and falling off to be carried away and dispersed by sea water. The other part remains attached to the parent plant and when its stalk dries and curves it is pushed into the sand. In this way it sends seeds to colonise new habitats but keeps some at home to replace the dying parent.

Many pioneers of beaches, like some of those described above, are trailing species that send out runners over the loose sand. The network of criss-crossing stems anchored by roots put down at intervals holds the sand and consolidates it. Such vegetation is usually sparse and appears to have only a precarious hold on its environment. Occasionally that hold slips and sand blows away, or is eroded by waves. The plants may live by virtue of the fact that they are anchored elsewhere, and they put down new roots from the runners, stubbornly renewing the battle against shifting sands.

With increasing deposition of sand, cays get larger and the plants in the centre become further removed from the sea. Sea birds begin nesting on the higher parts and fertilise the sand with guano, adding valuable nutrients, such as phosphates and nitrates. The sand, now stabilised by plants, receives organic matter in the form of decaying vegetation, and soil, rather than merely mineral sand, begins to develop. This creates conditions that allow plants other than pioneer species to grow. These are brought by sea birds, either clinging to their feathers, or in their digestive tracts. They take over in the central part of the island and form a lush carpet of herbs and grasses, leaving the pioneer species on the wind-swept, wave-battered shore.

In places the vegetation on coral cays can become quite lush, but may be swiftly reduced by drought and high tides.

The tar-vine, with its delicate flowers, grows well in soils that are rich in guano.

The chaff flower is also common to islands and cays and is distinguished by its slender spikes of reddish fruits.

Nightshade produces small purple fruit and is common to the islands.

CENTRAL VEGETATION

Tar-vine, *Boerhavia albiflora*, is characteristic of soils that are rich in guano. Its white-to-pinkish flowers are in small clusters. The seeds are sticky and tenaciously adhere to whatever they touch. Birds on islands where tar-vine grows often have numerous seeds clinging to their feathers. The taproot is large and fleshy and stores abundant food. It persists year after year, sending up new shoots that last a short while but then die back to be replaced by others. If conditions are unfavourable the plant can survive long periods of time on its stored food, continually sending out a few leaves to test the environment. Even when erosion exposes large portions of the roots, this species continues to survive, waiting for a better day.

Chaff flower, *Achyranthes aspera*, is a handsome plant distinguished by its slender spikes of reddish fruits. These cling to feathers and are dispersed by birds.

Nightshade, *Solanum nodiflorum*, subspecies *nutans*, a herb, produces purple fruits that are favoured by gulls and some land birds. After feeding on the fruits these birds' faeces are stained purple and contain many seeds. The seeds are carried to islands in the digestive tracts of such birds.

SHRUB RING

The next stage in the development of cay vegetation is the appearance of shrubs. At first there are only scattered shrubs around an island's edge, but gradually the gaps are filled and a shrub ring forms.

Octopus bush, *Argusia argentea*, has buoyant seeds that float for months and survive prolonged immersion in sea water. In fact, the seeds sprout better after soaking in salt water. They don't germinate while in the sea but only after being subsequently exposed to fresh water (rain) on some distant shore. It is a curious fact that these shrubs can disperse by sea thousands of kilometres but can't spread inland even a few metres! This is not because they can't grow inland. Small shrubs transplanted in the interior grow just as well as, or even better, than they do on the upper beach. It is simply that seeds falling beneath the parent tree or blowing inland haven't been treated in sea water and therefore don't germinate readily.

The sea lettuce tree, *Scaevola sericea*, is a shrub with shiny, bright green foliage. The white-to-purplish flowers are distinctively fan-shaped.

The sandpaper fig has a small fruit and is often found on the densely vegetated islands.

PARKLAND

Shrubs have important effects on a cay's ecology. They shelter the interior and protect it from wind and salt spray. This provides a new, more favourable environment for species of plants that could not survive there otherwise. Many of these are bird-dispersed, including species that come as seeds in the digestive tract. Some are herbs or grasses, but others are shrubs or trees. This mixture of herbs, grasses and trees that grows behind the shrub ring forms an open 'parkland'.

The sandpaper fig, *Ficus opposita*, is a species commonly found in parkland. It has rough leaves, a feature that gave rise to its common name, and produces a small fig as fruit. On some islands this species is very important because birds such as silver-eyes depend upon it at certain times of year.

The coastal she-oak, *Casuarina equisetifolia*, is also a common parkland tree, but is not restricted to that zone. Sometimes it grows in the shrub ring very close to the beach. It is not truly an oak, as suggested by its common name, nor a conifer as suggested by its appearance. In fact, its needle-like foliage is a growth of slender green stems with tiny scale-like leaves encircling them. The shade they cast and the gentle sound of the wind in their branches makes these trees a most welcome and pleasant species on an island.

The screw palm, *Pandanus* spp., is an unusual tree and is one of the most easily recognised species on the shores and islands of the Great Barrier Reef. It is sparingly branched and has tufts of palm-like foliage on the tip of each branch. The large, woody fruit is green when young but becomes orange at maturity, when it actually resembles a pineapple.

The peculiar screw palm is found on many islands and has a fruit which resembles a pineapple when it is ripe.

The coastal she-oak, or *Casuarina*, is common to parkland. It is noted for the gentle sound of the wind in its branches.

FOREST

The shrubs and trees in parkland lower the temperature of their area by casting shade. They also provide further protection from wind. Additional species now find conditions favourable for them to grow there. Eventually Pisonia trees, *Pisonia grandis*, become established and form a closed canopy casting dense shade. A heavy layer of leaf litter accumulates under the trees and the soil becomes rich and deep. Birds, especially the white-capped noddy, nest on the branches in large numbers, and shearwaters dig burrows in the forest floor. These birds add astounding amounts of guano to the soil. None of the pioneer species and few other plants can grow under the combined conditions of excess fertiliser and heavy shade found in Pisonia forest.

These central forests persist without further change for long periods of time unless some disruption occurs. They are sheltered by the shrub ring, and low pioneer vegetation persists on the unstable sands of the periphery.

Cays in all these stages of development can be seen on the Great Barrier Reef. Some are completely devoid of vegetation; others have only a sparse covering of pioneer species. Some have two zones, a central one of low plants and a peripheral one of pioneer species. Some are three-zoned, adding a partial or complete shrub ring. Then there are those that have the interior low vegetation replaced by parkland, and finally those like Masthead Island that have a number of concentric bands of vegetation with forest in the centre. Outside the forest is parkland, at least in places, surrounded by a shrub ring and finally a band of pioneer vegetation.

THREATS TO SURVIVAL

There are a number of environmental influences that alter the vegetation, in some cases leading to its damage or destruction. The most important agents of change are storms, erosion, wind, drought, sea turtles and seabirds.

Violent tropical storms, known in Australia as cyclones, are common in the Great Barrier Reef region and may do a lot of mechanical damage to islands and their vegetation. High waves crashing on the shore wash away large sections of beach, along with pioneer vegetation. In extreme cases whole cays may disappear. Even in storms of less ferocity, and in which the island's size and shape are unaltered, there may be considerable damage from washover by waves. After such storms wave-soaked plants die from excess salt.

Erosion often affects cays even when there aren't any storms. Onshore winds drive waves onto the beach and these undermine and wash away pioneer vegetation and sand. Erosion frequently cuts away the beach and eats its way into the central part of the island, leaving plants that do not normally grow near the edge forlornly hanging over a sagging sand bank.

Wind and weather have stripped this cay of all but one tiny clump of vegetation.

Erosion caused by storms and onshore winds usually results in the sand being deposited on the lee side. In this way an island may move progressively across a reef.

The eroded sand has to go somewhere. As the currents wash it around the cay it meets calmer waters in the lee and is deposited there, extending the beach on the side of the island opposite the erosion. In this way some islands move progressively across a reef, eroding on one side and redepositing the sand on the other. Beachrock, made of cemented sand, is formed only under beaches, and when an island moves a tell-tale outcrop of beachrock is often left behind, marking its former location. Unless prevailing wind directions or current patterns change, an island may eventually 'walk' off its reef to disappear into deep water. In the meantime, as the eroded beach retreats, the central vegetation can't keep up and appears to be displaced toward the edge of the eroding side. On the opposite side, wide new beaches are being formed and the pioneer vegetation is hard-pressed to colonise it as fast as it appears. Sometimes a shrub that used to be on the edge of a beach finds itself in the centre. The shrub has not moved, the island has moved around it! Even on relatively stable islands that do not wander around on their reefs, erosion has some effect. The beaches are always washed by waves and conditions are maintained that only pioneer species can sustain. The tips of islands are the most unstable and under long term time-lapse photography would seem to 'wobble'.

163

The succulent green vegetation (left) on One Tree Island was drastically affected by a drought and several years later it has still not recovered (right).

On broad expanses of open sand, such as on newly-forming beaches or those devastated by storms, there is little stabilising vegetation. The wind blows the sand along, piling it up into small dunes and covering plants. Sand can easily drift over the central vegetation in this way. On many islands the soil is layered into alternate dark and light bands. A dark band consists of sand in which vegetation was growing and depositing organic matter; the light band above it is made up of sand that blew in later.

Drought sometimes occurs on coral cays. A rather severe one took place during a long term study of One Tree Island, and killed more than half of the low vegetation. More importantly, the species most affected were those characteristic of the central area, whereas the pioneer plants survived well and eventually took over most of the cay. After the drought it was years before the original condition was restored. It seems that drought favours a return to pioneer vegetation at the expense of the species normally found in the centre.

Sea turtles dig nesting pits in the sand, digging up plants at the same time. When large numbers of turtles are nesting most of the vegetation in the nesting area may be mechanically uprooted. Some species die when they are exposed in this way. Pioneer species survive better, especially those that have long creepers. When part of the plant is dug up, there are often other parts somewhat distant that are still rooted and can support the uprooted parts until new roots can be put down. The overall effect the turtles have, then, is to maintain pioneer vegetation where they nest, often further inland than it would occur otherwise.

Seabirds can also have a damaging effect on vegetation. Many plants can't stand heavy accumulations of guano and die out in the vicinity of seabird nests. Seabirds also trample vegetation, killing it and preventing young plants from growing up.

CONTINENTAL ISLANDS

Continental islands, like cays, receive plants and animals over water, and lose them again by local extinction. But there is another dimension as well. Because continental islands are made of durable rock, rather than shifting sand, they are more stable and more permanent. Organisms find a more secure home there and perhaps persist longer.

Continental islands have kinds of habitats that cays lack. Cays have only sand and shingle, and soils derived from these, as substrates. In addition, continental islands have many of the same kinds of rocks as the mainland. These extra rock types provide different kinds of habitats and a greater number of them. For this reason plants and animals that could not survive on cays are able to inhabit continental islands.

Another important difference is that continental islands were once attached to the mainland and mainland species were present then. When the islands became isolated by rising sea levels or sinking land these species became marooned and the descendents of some of them have persisted to the present time. Many of these do not travel well over water and even if they could live on cays, could not reach them. As a result continental islands frequently have mainland species that one never finds on cays.

All of these reasons — greater permanence and stability, greater diversity of habitats, persistence of species from a former connection with the mainland — combine in causing the fauna and flora of continental islands to resemble those of the mainland. Nevertheless, continental islands are not just miniature mainlands. They have far fewer species than a chunk of the mainland of the same size. There are several reasons

Continental islands, such as Fitzroy Island (seen above), are made of durable rock and are therefore more permanent. Since they were once attached to the mainland many species are found there that do not exist on coral cays.

165

for this. One is that since they were separated from the mainland some of the species that do not travel well over water died out, for whatever reason, and haven't been able to make it back. Another is that they don't provide enough room for some of the bigger species. Large animals that require a lot of space would not have sufficient room on a small continental island to maintain a breeding population.

LAND REPTILES, AMPHIBIANS AND MAMMALS

Amphibians and mammals do not travel well over water and consequently they are seldom found on cays. In the Great Barrier Reef region, some cays have had goats in the past, some still have rats, and North West has feral domestic cats. All of these resulted from human introduction. Some of the inhabited continental islands have had the occasional wallaby introduced as a pet, but even these islands lack most of the larger Australian native mammals and have few species of the smaller ones. Amphibians and land mammals are the exception rather than the rule on islands of the Great Barrier Reef.

Most cays on the Reef lack land reptiles altogether, but a total of seven species (three skinks and four geckos) have been recorded from the area. All but the smallest of the continental islands have a few species of the more common coastal skinks, but certainly not a general representation of the species found in equivalent habitats on the mainland. A total of only 18 species of land reptiles, again mostly skinks and geckos, have been found from all of the islands collectively. Few islands have snakes and of the five species recorded, only one is venomous. Lizard Island is one

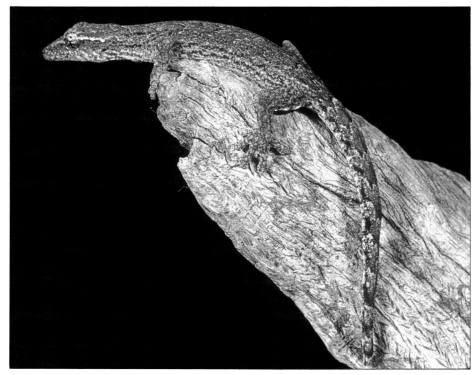

This gecko which is widely distributed on the reef islands is parthenogenetic, meaning that the female can lay fertile eggs without any contribution from a male.

166

of the larger continental islands and, as its name suggests, has lizards on it. In fact, it has most of the species of reptiles recorded from Barrier Reef Islands (ten species of lizards, four species of snakes) along with one species of frog.

Several species of geckos easily cross sea water and are distributed widely in the Pacific and Indian Oceans. One of them, *Lepidodactylus lugubris*, has sticky eggs which it lays in crevices in logs or under the bark of trees. When the newly-laid eggs dry they adhere tightly to the wood. The eggs are rather resistant to salt and it is likely that this species gets from island to island by eggs rafting in driftwood, as well as being transported by humans. It has another oddity. It is parthenogenetic, which means that females can lay fertile eggs without any contribution from a male. Males are completely absent, at least from some populations. Thus, even if only one animal reaches an island she can start a new population all by herself. It is perhaps one of the reasons this species is successful on islands, including some rather small cays. It took a long time to find out this amazing fact. Most people assumed they were ordinary lizards as they were frequently observed mating. However, it was later learned that these were lesbian mountings and didn't involve males at all.

B I R D S

Seabirds are a conspicuous part of the fauna of the Great Barrier Reef. Gulls and shorebirds walk along the beach, frigate birds soar high overhead and gannets, terns and shearwaters wheel over the waves to drop down on unsuspecting fish. There are 29 species of seabirds from seven different families in the region, of which 19 species breed there, with colonies on at least 78 different islands.

Islands of the Reef are sanctuaries for seabirds. There they can escape the ravages of mainland predators such as foxes, rats and the common household cat. This does not mean that seabirds have no worries on islands of the Great Barrier Reef. Silver

The masked gannet or masked booby is one of the most beautiful birds on the Reef. It nests mainly in winter and lays its eggs on the bare sand.

Nesting birds are frequently subject to attacks from gulls as evidenced by this broken egg.

gulls are always in attendance, always ready to dart in and break and eat an unguarded egg, or to carry off one of the helpless chicks. Terns, and even large species like gannets, must be constantly vigilant against such sneak attacks and are noticeably nervous when gulls approach.

Humans are unwitting allies of gulls in raids against other seabirds. When people approach, the relatively shy terns leave their nests; gulls waiting for just such a chance dart in and make short work of the nest contents, often unnoticed by the people inadvertently abetting them. Even a few visitors to an island, spread over the breeding season, can greatly influence the nesting success of seabirds. When humans are in residence or are frequent visitors to an island, ground-nesting seabirds seldom breed unless special precautions are taken not to disturb them.

The silver gull, *Larus novaehollandiae*, is one of the most conspicuous birds on the Reef as it is not shy of humans. Being a scavenger and predator it is quick to make use of scraps from ships or garbage dumps. The silver gull nests on the ground, usually among plants or on sand near some prominent object such as a piece of bleached coral or a drift log, and lays up to three dark-coloured eggs with black blotches. It is protective of its nest and relentlessly dives upon intruders and drives them away.

The brown booby or brown gannet, *Sula leucogaster*, doesn't coexist well with humans and seldom nests on mainlands. It is truly an insular species. It nests on the ground but usually adorns the site with a rude 'nest' of plants, shells, sponges, fish bones or even dried seasnakes. One or two (rarely three) eggs are laid, but only one chick is raised. A nearly-grown chick has such fluffy down that it appears larger than its parents. The adults take shifts, replacing each other as they alternately fish and guard the chick.

When not caring for young they may fly far from the nesting islands. Birds banded on the Great Barrier Reef have been recovered from such distant places as New Guinea, the Solomon Islands and Tasmania.

The masked gannet or masked booby, *Sula dactylatra*, is one of the most beautiful birds on the Reef. It nests on many of the small coral cays, often on the same ones as the brown booby. Nests of either species can be found at almost any time of the year, but the main breeding season of the brown booby is in summer, whereas breeding of the masked gannet peaks in winter. In that way they reduce some of the congestion that occurs on the islands they share. The masked gannet lays its eggs directly on bare sand well clear of vegetation and other debris, and doesn't construct a nest.

The white-breasted sea eagle, *Haliaetus leucogaster*, is the most majestic of seabirds, soaring high overhead along coasts and islands, swooping down to catch its prey of fish, seasnakes or other seabirds from the surface of the water. The adults are white with a grey back and young birds are mottled brown. Birds of this species nest in or among trees or tall man-made objects and consequently do not breed on islands with only low vegetation. They usually have a favourite, exposed perch where they sit to tear their prey apart.

They often use the same nest year after year, sometimes adding new material to it. One Tree Island, near the southern end of the Great Barrier Reef, has a nest on the ground in a clump of Pandanus trees. It was there when the naturalist J B Jukes visited the island in 1843 and was about the size then that it is today. It is colossal, measuring 2.35 metres high and 1.8 metres in diameter with the bowl almost 80 centimetres deep.

A brown booby keeps a watchful eye over its young. Although it may lay up to three eggs, only one chick is raised.

169

There are two species of frigatebirds on the Great Barrier Reef, the greater frigatebird, *Fregata minor*, and the lesser frigatebird, *Fregata ariel*. Both are similar but differ slightly in size and details of colouration. Adults are black and white, but the young have comic, unkempt red heads.

Frigatebirds are masters of the air, soaring lazily for hours without flapping their wings, attending to the adjustments of steering by precise movements of their deeply-forked tails. They feed and drink on the wing. They are pirates that chase other seabirds and bully them into dropping their prey, whereupon they swoop down and deftly catch their prize in mid-air.

The greater frigatebird usually nests in trees and the lesser frigatebird on low vegetation or bushes. Males in the breeding season have bright red, inflatable throat pouches.

The reef heron, *Egretta sacra*, is unusual because it comes in two colour varieties. Some are pure white except for the yellow beak and greenish-yellow legs. Others are leaden grey with a white throat. It seems to be a minor individual difference, like blue eyes and brown eyes in humans, both colour phases sometimes hatching from the same clutch of eggs. In some localities the white phase is the more common of the two; in others the grey phase is the more abundant. They nest on stick platforms built on the ground or in bushes or trees. They stalk their prey of molluscs, crustaceans and small fish by wading in shallow water or walking over the reef flat at low tide.

The wedge-tailed shearwater or muttonbird, *Puffinus pacificus*, has solid dark plumage and is a skilful flier. It is seldom seen except on the wing at sea, for on land it occupies burrows in the soil, where it also nests. When searching for its food of small fish and various floating and surface-living organisms, it manoeuvres wingtip to wave crest over the surface of the water, often being lost to view in the troughs of waves.

The mutton bird is rarely seen except on the wing. It migrates over vast distances and is a skilful flier.

The white-capped noddy, seen here with its chick, is very tame and nests in the crook of trees on larger islands.

The lesser frigate bird nests on low vegetation, as on Bell Cay, Swain Reefs.

Many tourists know it mainly from its voice. During the breeding season, ghostly wailings and moanings, more reminiscent of pain and distress than of passion, waft from their nuptial burrows much of the night.

There are two very similar species of noddies on the Great Barrier Reef. Both are uniformly dark except for a white cap on the head. They differ mainly in body and size and in brightness of the cap. The common noddy, *Anous stolidus*, nests on the ground, often on small islands. The white-capped noddy, *Anous minutus*, is a favourite, not only for its slender, graceful build and beauty, but because it is so tame, taking little notice of humans even at close range. Its nests are in trees and are elaborately constructed from leaves and other materials.

There are many kinds of terns on the Great Barrier Reef, all predominantly white or light grey with black markings on the head, especially on the crown. These are the fast-flying birds that one often sees in flocks diving upon schools of small fish forced to surface by larger predators beneath. Many are social and carry out their activities in groups. They nest in dense colonies, often holding raucous congresses at their breeding grounds.

A number of species of sandpipers, plovers, dotterels, turnstones, whimbrels and other shorebirds can be seen on the beaches of mainland or offshore islands. They walk along singly or in small groups, inquisitively pecking at anything that is potential

171

food. Many of these birds are merely visitors making stopovers in their transcontinental migratory flights, or are tourists spending the winter here before returning to their native Siberia, or other equally distant parts, to breed. Consequently, they are not dressed for the occasion and are in drab, non-breeding plumage. Some of the species look very much alike at this time of year and it takes a dedicated bird-watcher to tell them apart.

The oystercatchers are the most distinctive and conspicuous of the shorebirds, with black plumage, red bills and red or pink legs. They are large birds, and wander along beaches or on mudflats, usually in pairs, looking for small marine animals. There are two species in the Great Barrier Reef region — the sooty oystercatcher, *Haematopus fuliginosus*, which is dark all over, and the pied oystercatcher, *Haematopus ostralegus*, which has a white underside.

Continental islands, unlike cays, have a variety of land birds. That is not to say that few land birds reach the cays. Many do, but find these small islands unsuitable for their nesting or other requirements. Indeed, migrants, stray individuals or irregular visitors are frequently seen on cays. For example, One Tree Island has had 20 species recorded from it, but only two of those are permanent residents which breed there. The rest were merely individuals that briefly visited the island and then went elsewhere.

The land birds most commonly resident on coral islands are banded rails and silver-eyes. The banded rail, *Rallus philippensis*, is a handsome brownish-to-reddish bird with a banded chest and abdomen and a white stripe above the eye. It is found on many islands, not only on the Great Barrier Reef but in the eastern Indian Ocean and south-western Pacific Ocean as well. Few species of land birds stay on cays that have only low vegetation as most require trees for nesting. The banded rail is an exception. Although it also lives on islands with trees and even on mainland coasts; it can inhabit remarkably small islands with only low plants; it nests on the ground. Sometimes the resident population is only a few breeding pairs. Rails are shy and one seldom catches more than a glimpse of a small bird, shaped somewhat like a chicken, darting from one clump of vegetation to another. They seldom take to the wing. However, on islands where humans live and do not molest them they may become quite tame.

The grey-breasted silver-eye, *Zosterops lateralis chlorocephala*, is a common land bird on the Bunker and Capricorn Islands. It is a tiny greenish-grey bird with a yellowish tinge and a conspicuous white ring around the eye. It eats insects and fruits and, on some islands, it depends on the fruits of the sandpaper fig at certain times of the year.

The numbers of seabirds nesting on small cays is truly astounding. There are 20 000 sooty terns, *Sterna fuscata*, nesting on Michaelmas Cay and 10 000 on Raine Island (along with 12 other species); 70 000 white-capped noddies nest on Heron Island and 160 000 on North West Island. In addition, 8000 common noddies nest

A flock of terns takes off from Price Cay. These fast flying birds nest in dense colonies on many parts of the Reef.

on Michaelmas Cay and 6000 on North Reef Cay on Frederick Reef. The breeding population of wedge-tailed shearwaters on North West Island is 750 000!

Some of the cays are more important breeding grounds than others. The ten most important ones on the Great Barrier Reef, in descending order, are Raine, Bramble, Michaelmas, Swain Reefs (a number of tiny cays), Masthead, North West, One Tree, Wilson, Pipon and Fairfax. Tourism has meant that some of these are being developed too heavily and breeding populations of the more sensitive birds are likely to decline, if not disappear altogether.

SEA TURTLES

Sea turtles lay eggs in mainland beaches but, like seabirds, they find islands safe havens for nesting. Various islands and cays support important breeding activity. On the shallow reefs around cays one can often get a glimpse of a turtle swimming along, or with its head raised above water to take a breath. They are most easily observed, however, when females laboriously struggle up a beach to lay their eggs. Their brief sojourn ashore is marked by a characteristic track, soon to be obliterated by the changing tides.

Once a female has selected a suitable nest site, she uses her back flippers to excavate a deep nest chamber into which she lays up to 100 or more eggs resembling table tennis balls. She then covers them with sand and tamps it with her bottom shell, finally to slide back under the waters from whence she came, leaving her eggs to develop on their own in their moist sandy cavern. She may repeat this performance three to five times at about fortnightly intervals during a single breeding season, but after that not breed again for a number of years.

The mother's choice of a nest site is most important. The conditions under which eggs develop determine much about their future. If the sand is too dry, too wet or too salty they may not develop properly or they may die. If they are too close to the sea they may be washed out and destroyed by tides. If the sand is too cool (below 24°C) or too hot (above 34°C) they will not hatch.

One of the truly amazing things about sea turtles is that sex is not genetically determined as it is in humans and many other animals. The temperature at which the embryos develop determines what sex they will become! Within the tolerance

A loggerhead turtle digs a pit in which she will lay up to 100 or more eggs before slipping back into the water.

174

A turtle's tracks in the sand at Frigate Cay reveal the exact location of the pit in which she has laid her eggs.

limits mentioned above, those that develop in warm nests become females whereas those that develop in cool ones become males. The actual cut-off point differs slightly among species.

This method of sex determination is important for conservation of sea turtles. It could be disastrous for turtles if a reserve set aside for them had only cool beaches where only males were produced, while nearby warmer female-producing beaches were allowed to be used for purposes incompatible with turtle nesting.

The egg-laying of sea turtles is fascinating, and can be observed at close range. The female is shy at first and will return to the water if disturbed by humans. Once she has finished her nest and begun to lay her eggs however, she seems to pay no attention to an invasion of her privacy and continues with her maternal tasks.

Often tears stream down her face while she is laying her eggs. She doesn't cry, as was once believed, because of the responsibilities of motherhood, or because she is reflecting on the future dangers of her young as they begin their precarious existence in a hostile world. She is probably oblivious to all of that. Rather the tears are salty and are her way of getting rid of the excess salt she takes in from her marine environment since her kidneys are totally inadequate to cope with the heavy salt loads imposed by living in sea water.

175

It is partly a matter of luck whether one sees a turtle laying eggs. Nesting occurs on the Great Barrier Reef from November until February, but the number laying eggs varies greatly from year to year. The largest number ever recorded was over 11 000 females coming ashore on one night along a beach only 1.7 kilometres long during the peak of the 1974–75 nesting season at Raine Island! Such heavy traffic was a disadvantage to the turtles, as the beach was so congested that they dug up previous nests in the process of digging their own pit. Many eggs were accidentally destroyed in this way.

Most sea turtles lay their eggs at night and one has to walk the beaches, sometimes in the early hours of the morning to witness the event. One species, the loggerhead, is more obliging and often trundles ashore in broad daylight.

When the young hatch they dig their way to the surface and suddenly 'boil' out of the sand and make a dangerous trek to the sea, often accompanied by crabs and gulls or other predatory birds that may take a heavy toll. Once in the sea they are still not safe as sharks and other fish wait just offshore to snap them up. It is good luck if even one or two out of 1000 survive to the age of 50 years, when they first begin to breed.

The sea turtles of the Great Barrier Reef are inveterate travellers. Turtles tagged by marine biologists have been recovered from many places far from where they originally received the tag. Instead, many of the turtles that breed on the Reef migrate to feeding grounds in countries up to 2000 kilometres distant, often across deep oceanic water. The next time they breed they make the return trip.

It is still a mystery why they travel such long distances, only to return time after time to breed on the same or nearby beach. The greatest mystery of all is where turtles of intermediate sizes go. When tiny hatchlings leave the nest and enter the sea, it is as though they are swallowed up. They are not seen again until they have reached the size of large dinner plates. Where have they been for the intervening time? And what did they do? No one knows.

There are seven species of sea turtles in the world, six of which occur in Australian waters. Four of these are a regular part of the fauna of the Great Barrier Reef or the waters between the Reef and the Queensland coast. The green turtle, *Chelonia mydas*, is the most abundant turtle on the Reef. It is olive green to brownish above when adult, but the hatchlings are nearly black. Many of them live year round on the Reef and breed on islands there. In addition, large numbers have feeding grounds elsewhere, such as the Arafura Sea and Coral Sea, or even further afield, but return to Barrier Reef islands to lay eggs. In many parts of the world this species is heavily exploited by man for meat and eggs.

The loggerhead turtle, *Caretta caretta*, is somewhat larger than the green turtle, and is brown to yellowish above. It has a head that appears somewhat too large for the rest of its body. The loggerhead inhabits lagoons on the Reef and inshore bays of the mainland, but breeds mainly on the cays of the Capricornia Section of the Reef or adjacent mainland. Loggerheads from the Coral and Arafura seas also come to nest there.

The hawksbill, *Eretmochelys imbricata*, is very distinctive, and smaller than the other Australian sea turtles. Its upper jaw has a downward point giving it the appearance of having a beak like a hawk — hence its name. The shell is olive brown to brown above, richly variegated with reddish brown, dark brown or black. When polished the shell is handsome and is the source of commercial tortoise-shell. This species is found in limited numbers throughout the Great Barrier Reef. It lays eggs on small cays in the northern part of the Reef or Torres Strait, or migrates as far away as the Solomon Islands.

The flatback, *Natator depressa*, has, as its name suggests, a fairly flat shell. Unlike other sea turtles that travel internationally, the flatback lives only in Australia, never leaving the shallow water of the continental shelf. It nests mainly on beaches of continental islands. Although present in the Great Barrier Reef region, it is not usually found on the Reef itself.

The other two Australian sea turtles are not often seen in the Reef region. Occasionally the olive ridley, *Lepidochelys olivacea*, is seen in the turbid waters inshore of the Reef, but no one knows where these breed. The leatherback, *Dermochelys coriacea*, occurs in all temperate and tropical seas but is seldom seen near the Reef.

MANGROVES

Mangrove forests blur the boundary between land and sea. Along quiet shorelines they creep seaward, their gracefully arching aerial roots giving them the appearance of tip-toeing into the water with raised skirts. Behind this vanguard stand more solidly rooted trees, only wetting their feet at high tide. Finally, there are land-based ones that merely squelch in soggy soil.

These trees are not just of one kind. Indeed, about 30 species of trees and shrubs from 14 different families of flowering plants in the Australian region are considered to be mangroves. It is their habit of living in salty wetlands that define these trees as mangroves.

Mangroves grow quickly on many parts of the Reef. There are many species and they are noted for their ability to thrive in salty wetlands.

Because different kinds of plants have invaded this habitat, they have adapted to it in different ways. Consider, for example, the problem of getting air to roots submerged in water or embedded in waterlogged soil. Some mangroves have solved this problem by having aerial roots or stilt roots that leave the trunk of the tree well above high water level; these roots can breathe through the parts that aren't submerged. Other mangroves have roots leaving the tree underground but sending up finger-like projections called pneumatophores that protrude above water level, like snorkels, to obtain air. In still others the root grows upwards from the soil, then downward again, leaving a knee-shaped section sticking above the soil or water. These are appropriately called knee-roots. Some species that do not grow in standing water, but merely waterlogged soil, lack any specialisation of the roots. Rather, their roots run along the surface of the wet soil where the tops at least are exposed to air.

Or take the problem of too much salt. Some mangroves absorb sea water through the roots and then excrete the excess salt, leaving the fresh water behind. Such trees have encrustations of salt on the leaf surfaces left there by brine from special salt-secreting glands in the leaves. Other mangrove species can prevent salt from entering the roots, allowing only water in. Finally, some species neither secrete salt nor keep it from entering the roots. They have merely become tolerant to high salt levels and have salty tissues.

One feature of the seascape to which mangroves haven't adjusted is wave action. For that reason they are found on sheltered coasts, in secluded inlets or along the edges of estuaries. There rich organic mud can settle and accumulate without being washed away. One of the main characteristics of mangrove forest is copious, thick mud which provides nutrients, not only for the trees but also for many kinds of crabs, molluscs, fish and other animals that live there. Indeed, mangroves are essential breeding grounds for a number of commercially-important fish.

Whereas mud and mangroves are intimately linked, mud and corals are incompatible. Sediments cover up coral polyps and they die. Rivers that discharge silt usually have little or no coral growing near their mouths. Along the Queensland coast reefs and mangroves both abound, but usually in different situations, the mangroves occurring in muddy estuaries and the corals in clear, clean water. There are a few instances where mangroves and corals do grow in close proximity. Some of the larger continental islands on the Great Barrier Reef have mangroves along their shores. Others, known as Complex Wooded Isles, have one or more shingle banks protecting the reef top on the windward side and a sand cay on the leeward side. Mangroves grow in the calm, shallow water sheltered between the two. There are also a few islands of only mangroves growing on shallow reef tops where tidal range is small.

Dispersal of all species of mangrove trees is by sea. In some, individual seeds are buoyant but in others it is the entire fruit that floats. Some mangroves have a unique means of dispersal. The seeds germinate while still on the parent tree and the embryo begins to grow. It is the young plant that falls from the tree into the water and either floats away to grow wherever currents and tides may take it, or takes root in the mud beneath its parent. All of these propagules, seeds, fruits and seedlings are common sights along the beaches of islands, even those on which no mangroves grow.

There are gradients in many conditions from the sea shoreward, including salinity, the amount of waterlogging and organic matter. Because different species of mangrove have different requirements and tolerances, they tend to sort out along this gradient into rather distinct zones. In the region of the Great Barrier Reef there are five such zones.

Different types of mangroves have variable tolerances of salinity and moisture. This aerial photograph dramatically illustrates the different zones of growth of the various mangrove species.

The most seaward zone is the Seaward Fringe. Only a few pioneer species grow there, taking the full brunt of seaward conditions and sheltering the zones further toward land. One of the main species in this zone is the hardy, widespread Avicennia, *Avicennia marina*. Growth is difficult there and seedlings are often covered by mud and barnacles. The next most inward zone is named the Rhizophora zone after the major species occurring there, the stilt mangrove, *Rhizophora stylosa*. This zone is characterised by a nearly impenetrable tangle of proproots, embedded in deep mud and bathed by advancing and retreating tides. It is the image most people bring to mind when mangrove swamps are mentioned. Behind this zone is the majestic Bruguiera zone, a magnificent closed forest with trees sometimes reaching up to 30 metres in height. It is dominated by the orange mangrove, *Bruguiera gymnorhiza*. This zone is behind standing water and the soil is firmer and less salty than in the two preceding zones. Behind the Bruguiera zone is a low, shrubby thicket-like zone dominated by the yellow mangrove, *Ceriops tagal*. This is called the Ceriops zone, where there are often bare areas of salty soil. Finally, there is a Landward zone

The stilt mangroves above form a tangle of roots in deep mud. It is this seemingly impenetrable barrier that is the image most people have of mangrove swamps.

that contains a number of different mangrove species, even including some of those from other zones, such as the Avicennia from the Seaward Fringe. The Landward zone grades into more typical land vegetation such as rainforest in areas of high rainfall, or drier forests, woodland, or even grassland where rainfall is lower.

Nature does not follow blueprints and the rather ideal scheme portrayed here is not always realised. There are many exceptions and particular zones may be missing. There may not be a Seaward Fringe but rather the outer zone may be mainly of stilt mangroves, or the Bruguiera zone may grade directly into rainforest, and so on. As one gets away from the tropics most of this disappears until only one species, Avicennia, is left.

The taller mangroves, called *Bruguiera gymnorhiza*, which grow in firmer soil, form closed forests with trees often reaching up to 30 metres.

DIVING ON THE GREAT BARRIER REEF

MARK GOYEN

As the dive boat drops anchor on the first reef on this, the first day of the dive expedition, the crisp dawn air greets the diver, woken from a night of often broken sleep. Beneath the boat, fish swim to and fro. Gentle waves break against a coral rampart making the music of the Reef. Equipment is wrested from the gear tub, checked and made ready. A splash, the sound and feel of bubbles and then the vista is everywhere. A plethora of life, of beauty and the vibrant rhythm of the greatest display of underwater energy on the planet; the Great Barrier Reef unfolds.

A white-tip reef shark scurries from the intruder. Clown fish aggressively gape at their reflections in the diver's face-mask. Chaetodons flit away. Parrotfish follow in the wake of the diver's fins hoping for some morsel or scrap. For any diver, this is pure delight.

Sunset comes. The fading light signals a change of shifts for the creatures of the Reef and new opportunities for the exploring diver.

A diver 'floats' down to find a world of corals, soft and hard.

SCUBA divers in Australia have a special relationship with the Great Barrier Reef. As a group, we are in an enviable position to explore the wonders of the underwater environment; to us it is a source of pride and by some it is even seen as a birthright. Trainee divers in the cities often express a longing to get to the Reef, to see the best that the world of diving has to offer. To the diving population, awareness of the Reef is even more acute than to the general Australian public. Its health is an important issue and being able to enjoy it in the future is a constant concern. Divers seek solace in the fact that they know it is there.

A sense of flying over rolling fields can be exhilarating. A vista of branching corals.

To the diver, then, what are the features of the Great Barrier Reef that make it unique? Its vastness, the variety of its living things, its moods, its unpredictability, the scope for exploration and discovery . . . the list goes on. Within these 2 000 kilometres there exists every type of dive and dive experience. To put it simply, the Reef has everything. Shipwrecks, spectacular cliff-like coral precipices and drop-offs, 100 metre visibility, sharks, whales, huge schools of pelagic fish, spectacular gardens of corals in pristine condition. It is small wonder that almost every diver ranks his or her time on the Reef as the best, a benchmark against which all other experiences are measured.

The history of diving on the Great Barrier Reef begins at the turn of the last century. It is a short, fascinating and now rapidly changing story of the discovery of a glorious asset.

The earliest use of commercial diving equipment in the north of Australia was in the pearling and trochus shell diving industries of Thursday Island and Broome. Short careers and life-spans were very common in these divers. Severe decompression sickness was common and equipment extremely bulky and unreliable. Still, the industry was substantial and obviously quite lucrative.

Collecting sea-slugs from the sandy floors between reefs may seem an unlikely source of income, but it too has been an industry along the northern sections of the Great Barrier Reef. Dried sea-slugs, or bêche-de-mer, have an important place in Chinese and Eastern cooking and medicine. Perhaps the diver had the best of things here, at least underwater, being spared the stench of a few thousand of these creatures drying above the deck of the boat.

The end of the 1940s and the beginning of the '50s saw the emergence of the pioneers of the modern era in reef exploration and discovery. Amongst these was Noel Monkman, adventurer and cinematographer, a diver who initially used hard-hat technology but was quick to understand the significance of a self-contained underwater breathing apparatus (SCUBA). With this and camera in hand he was able to captivate an audience fascinated and intimidated by the mysteries of the Reef.

Early newspaper articles on the Reef and diving magazines in general concentrated on the dangerous, the bizarre and the exploits of a few hardy adventurers rather than attempting to understand or appreciate this complex ecosystem. Reports of fish slaughters with spearguns were made with pride. The environment was seen as something to be tamed by conquering its larger inhabitants; a common thread in the history of exploration and a comment on the human condition.

It was not until the early '70s that this trend was reversed, a change of heart that surprisingly has often been championed by some of those at the forefront of the slaughter. A conservationist and enlightened attitude has helped develop Australia's magnificent coast of coral into a joy for the SCUBA diver, with many purpose-built dive boats, dive stores and dive instruction facilities. The opportunity now exists to explore the whole of the Queensland coast from almost any point.

The boat is anchored and the dive begins.

It is estimated that, on average, at any one time of day there are over 1000 people snorkelling and SCUBA diving on the Great Barrier Reef. Such numbers would have been unthinkable as little as a decade ago.

The facilities available during the early days of SCUBA were extremely primitive compared to those enjoyed today although there is little documented evidence. Amongst the most articulate recollections of a generation ago are those of Arthur C. Clarke in *A Coast of Coral*. Arthur Clarke, smitten by the new technology and freedom of SCUBA, journeyed along the Queensland coast in the mid '50s. He describes the inadequacies of the Queensland railway system with a poignancy that few travel writers could emulate. Today, thankfully, such problems are largely avoidable.

In some ways the progress of diving as an activity along the Great Barrier Reef mirrors the general economic development and sophistication of Queensland itself. Just as sugar cane and mining led to the growth of large service towns along the coast, so too do they determine the starting points for expeditions to the Reef and the most dived areas. Thus the focus of diving around the Townsville area centres on reefs within a convenient range of the city. The fact that the Yongala wreck is within the scope of one to two day tours from this port is a happy coincidence and not the *raison d'etre* of the dive operations in the area. With the exception of the coast north of Cooktown, however, the spacing of major centres does provide for good access to the reefs.

A surprised puffer fish fills with water and pretends to be a much bigger fish than he is.

The present day is a superb time to experience the Reef. While some islands and resorts provide the utmost in comfort, luxury and elegance, it is still possible to find adventure and diving on remote untouched reefs, and even to spend ten days at sea without sighting another vessel.

In recent years there has been an exponential growth in the number of facilities for divers. This has streamlined the arrangement of dive trips and provided many more opportunities for visitors to view the Reef as it should be seen. Here are some suggestions for divers of all levels of experience.

1. Day Trips

A number of dive operators now have day trips to areas of the Reef from nearby ports. Cairns and Port Douglas, due to their proximity to the Reef proper, are major spots for these 'two tank trips'. This type of diving is ideal for the diver who has a limited budget, little time or both. Most dive sites on day trips tend to be inner reefs, so visibility should not be expected to be as predictable or good as outer reefs.

Many of the resort islands in the Whitsunday group offer high speed boats to outer reefs and, if cost is of no consequence, air charter companies provide divers with transport to off-shore platforms and some great underwater experiences.

2. Dive Cruise Trips

Pick up any diving magazine in Australia, or for that matter in the world, and there will be many advertisements for 'live-aboard' diving vessels. For the serious diver, there is little doubt that this type of diving is the best available. The best and most remote sites can be reached and in general it is possible simply to jump off the stern of the boat onto the dive site. The crews of these boats are usually composed of experienced and enthusiastic divers and three and sometimes more dives (including night dives) are possible per day. On a cost per dive basis a 'live aboard' dive vessel is often much cheaper than staying at an island resort or on the mainland.

There are special diving boats operating from all major centres along the Queensland coast but in the peak season, October to late December, it is often difficult to secure a booking, so it is important to plan well ahead.

Some diving locations can only be reached in this way. Of particular importance are the reefs of the Coral Sea, both the northern and southern sections, and the vast reef complexes of the Swain reefs, Saumarez reefs and the Pompey complex to the south. Divers who love excitement and magnificent visibility can dream about an expedition far into the Coral Sea, taking in such magical reefs as Marion, Abington, Flinders, Holmes, Bougainville and Osprey, an epic journey almost half the length of the Queensland coast.

Culcita novaeguinae, the pincushion starfish. As hard as a rock and coming in a multitude of colours this unusual starfish is interrupted from its meal of coral.

Blue skies and bright sunlight. The water is so clear a diver contemplates the need for shade.

At Pixie Pinnacle a meal is offered – and accepted – from every side.

3. RESORT HOLIDAYS

For some divers a resort holiday represents the ideal combination — of comfort, proximity to the Reef and excellent diving. For variety, diving and non-diving activities can be combined and this type of holiday is often ideal for families.

Heron Island has always been an extremely popular location for a reef island holiday. A coral cay formed by an ever changing deposit of sand resulting from the breakdown of algal and coral skeletons, the island is surrounded by reefs which offer excellent diving, including its famous Bommie. Lady Elliot Island, the southernmost island of the Great Barrier Reef, is also an ideal location for this type of holiday.

Much further north, Lizard Island, a continental island, provides many dive sites and the famous Cod Hole is only a few miles due east.

While the Whitsunday group is very picturesque, in general the diving around the islands is done in quite shallow water, with variable and often restricted visibility due to their close proximity to the mainland. A trip to the outer reef from these islands (up to two hours away, by high speed boat) will generally produce better conditions.

The potato cod is a large predator. Man and beast are nearer rivals here – neither is threatened, both are inquisitive.

190

4. ISLAND CAMPING

It is possible to arrange a camping holiday on a Barrier Reef island or to book on an organised excursion to an island with a semi-permanent camping area and community. The most popular islands for this sort of diving activity are in the Capricorn and Bunker groups to the south, notably North West and Lady Musgrave islands. Many dive sites are accessible by walking over the reef flat, although a small boat or inflatable is a tremendous asset.

Camping on most islands is strictly controlled by the Queensland National Parks and Wildlife Service and a permit must be obtained from one of their regional offices.

Low cost is the major advantage of this type of expedition, but the peace and serenity of an undeveloped environment is particularly memorable.

5. LEARNING TO DIVE ON THE REEF

A holiday where one can acquire a new skill is a great attraction for many people. Learning to dive is not only an exceptional experience, it also gives an entree to the world's most beautiful underwater environment.

Most mainland cities, notably Cairns and Townsville, the entrepots for many overseas visitors, have dive schools as do many island resorts. Courses usually take at least four days of reasonably simple but time-consuming study and practical work. The early practical sessions are done in a pool or very shallow sandy reef flat and not on reefs. At the end of the course a basic diving certificate is issued and, as with all of the courses undertaken in Australia, this certificate is recognised world-wide.

In the north where food is abundant and disturbances are few, soft corals can grow to enormous sizes.

191

6. Snorkelling and Other Activities

Almost without exception SCUBA divers start the sport as breathe-hold divers. Even today, of the people who come to see the Great Barrier Reef, the majority will not proceed past this level. Still, much can be enjoyed from the surface and by shallow diving. Snorkel divers are catered for by specialist tour operators along the length of the coast and at most island resorts. Accompanying non-SCUBA divers on such excursions is often as great a thrill for the long-standing diver as for the beginners themselves.

The number of underwater observatories and aquariums in and around tourist centres and islands is increasing. Townsville has a beautiful display of marine life in a 'walk-under' aquarium and near to Cairns is the well-established observatory on Green Island.

One of the most exciting prospects for the future though, is the use of one atmosphere diving suits and small submersibles capable of deep exploration to depths of 300 metres and beyond. Such excursions will add an extra dimension to diving for SCUBA and snorkel divers alike.

The following are the major locations corresponding to areas of the Great Barrier Reef Marine Park and the coastal transport network and service towns. It is important to remember that only a select area of the Reef can be experienced in any one trip and hard decisions about what to do and where to go are best made well in advance, unless the diver has absolutely no restrictions. Perhaps the most important factor is deciding just how much diving to do.

A diver swims between two worlds – the reef and the depths. Strong upwelling currents in such places bring food to the forest of whip corals along the drop off.

Ancient walls of coral soar towards the surface at 'the cathedral', Wishbone Reef in the far north.

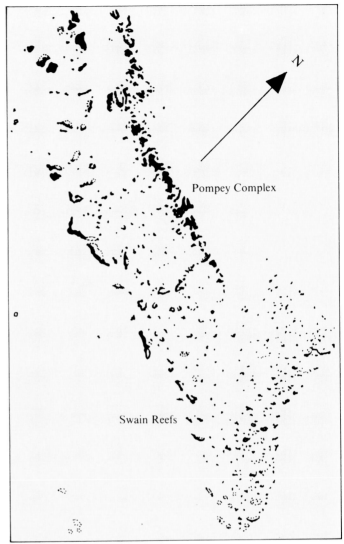

SWAIN REEFS, SAUMAREZ REEFS AND POMPEY
COMPLEX

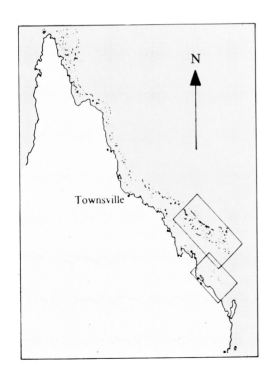

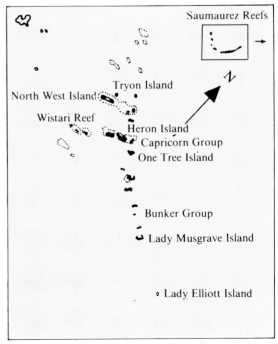

THE TROPIC OF CAPRICORN

194

THE MAJOR DIVING AREAS OF THE GREAT BARRIER REEF

1. AROUND THE TROPIC OF CAPRICORN

Major Island Group and Reefs	Capricorn and Bunker Groups Great Keppel Island
Access Ports	Gladstone (Capricorn Group) Bundaberg (Bunker Group)
Diving Attractions	HERON ISLAND. The Heron Island 'Bommie' renowned for its huge population of tame fish which divers have been hand feeding for a quarter of a century. Marine Research station. Excellent resort and dive facilities. LADY ELLIOT ISLAND. The massive forms of huge manta rays are frequently sighted at Lighthouse Reef. GREAT KEPPEL ISLAND. Many types of sea snakes are very common at the dive sites.
Best Diving Season	October to mid January.
Diving Organisation	Heron, Lady Elliot and Great Keppel resorts. Numerous dive charter boats. Cruises usually one week or more, visiting a number of islands. Extensions to the Swain Reefs are possible. Camping. It is possible to camp on many of these islands. A permit is required and, unless part of a group, considerable organisation is needed.

2. SWAIN, SAUMAREZ REEFS, POMPEY COMPLEX

Major Reefs	Swain Reefs, Saumarez Reefs, Pompey Complex. Due to the vast distances required to reach these destinations, any trip will be at least a week-long.
Access Ports	Gladstone, Yeppoon (Swain, Saumarez Reefs) Yeppoon, Mackay (Pompey Complex)
Diving Attractions	At present none of these locations are regularly dived and each voyage is really an expedition of discovery. SWAIN REEFS. Pelagic fish, sharks, large numbers of sea-snakes. Gannet Cay is inhabited only by sea birds. SAUMAREZ REEFS. Good visibility, shark sightings. POMPEY COMPLEX. Recently, a number of blue holes have been found in this intricate reef network. Some are 50 metres or more across, a similar depth and will no doubt be a source of great interest in years to come.
Best Diving Season	During settled weather from October to January.
Diving Organisation	Only on live-aboard dive boats on pre-booked excursions.

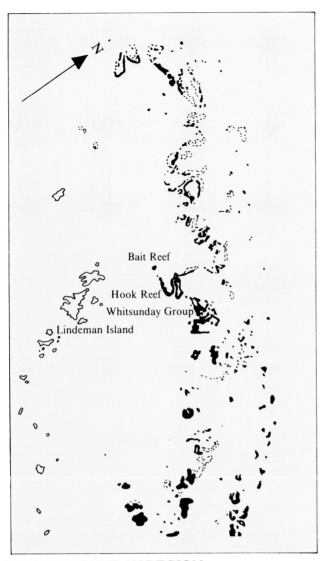

THE WHITSUNDAY REGION

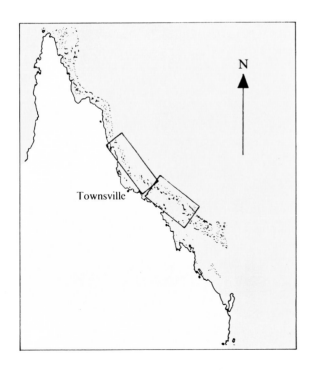

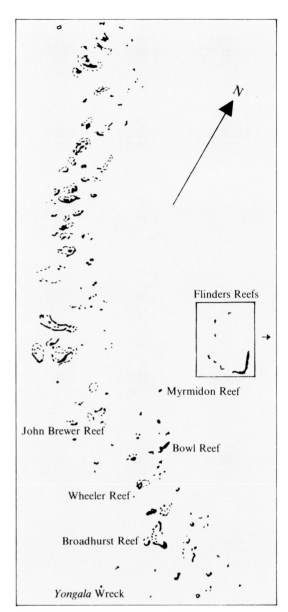

TOWNSVILLE AREA AND
THE SOUTHERN CORAL SEA

3. THE WHITSUNDAY REGION

Major Reefs	Reefs surrounding continental islands — Hamilton, Hayman, Lindeman, Daydream, South Molle islands. Outer reefs north-east of the island resorts — Bait, Black, Hardy, Line, Hook and other reefs.
Access Ports	Proserpine is the major township. Airlie Beach. Shute Harbour.
Diving Attractions	CONTINENTAL ISLAND REEFS. Occasionally good, but inconsistent diving. Proximity to coast restricts underwater visibility. OUTER REEFS. Generally preferred by divers. Access by fast 'day-trip' boats taking one to two hours each way. Bait Reef, the closest, is the most dived site.
Best Diving Season	October to early January. As most accommodation is shore based, winter winds are less of a problem.
Diving Organisation	Day trip diving boats are most common. Some larger vessels combine diving with Whitsunday Island cruising. Snorkelling as part of a sailing holiday on ten to 15 metre vessels.

4. TOWNSVILLE AREA AND THE SOUTHERN CORAL SEA

Major Reefs	TOWNSVILLE AREA. Numerous reefs are dived with Townsville as a base for Shrimp and Viper Reefs in the south to Myrmidon Reef in the north. YONGALA WRECK. 80 kilometres south of Townsville. SOUTHERN CORAL SEA. Encompasses a huge area. Flinders Reef is the closest and most often dived; nearby is Dart Reef. Marion Reef, to the south, is much closer to Mackay.
Access Ports	Townsville. Mackay (Marion Reef)
Diving Attractions	S.S. YONGALA WRECK, the highlight of almost any expedition in this area. MYRMIDON REEF. Excellent visibility WHEELER REEF. Hand-feeding of white-tip reef sharks. FLINDERS REEF. Visibility up to 50 metres is common. Pelagic fish common. MARION REEF. Spectacular visibility, coral pinnacles, sharks.
Best Diving Season	October to mid January.
Diving Organisation	All diving is done from live-aboard dive boats as distances travelled are large and there are no nearby islands.

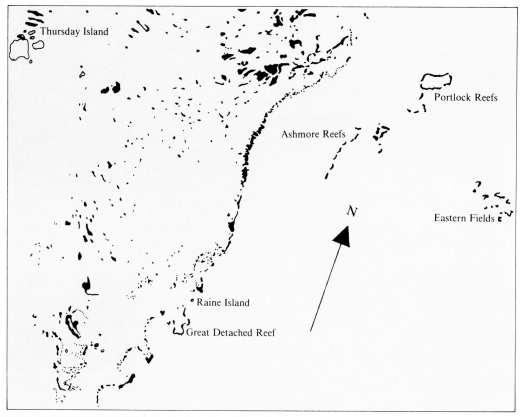

THE NORTHERN REEF AND NORTHERN CORAL SEA

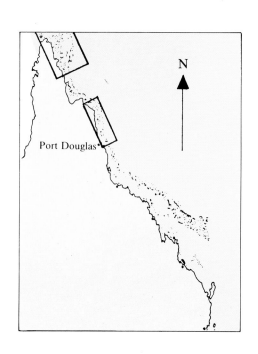

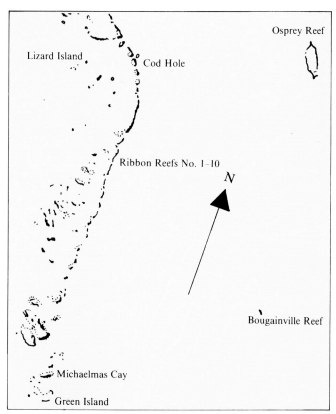

CAIRNS AND LIZARD ISLAND REGION

5. CAIRNS, LIZARD ISLAND REGION

Major Reefs	Local Cairns and Port Douglas reefs
	Ribbon Reefs
	Lizard Island
	The Cod Hole
	Osprey Reef
Access Ports	Cairns
	Port Douglas
Diving Attractions	LOCAL CAIRNS AND PORT DOUGLAS REEFS. Here the outer reef hugs the coast and there is plenty of excellent diving, less than an hour from shore.
	RIBBON REEFS. These are thin strands of reef numbered one to ten extending north of Port Douglas to Lizard Island. The landward corners of the gaps in the reefs are the most dived. Pixie Pinnacle and Dynamite Passage are favourites. 500 metre drop-offs are on the seaward side, but can be dived only in perfect conditions.
	LIZARD ISLAND. Some excellent dives around the island close to the resort.
	THE COD HOLE. This is at the northern extremity of the Ribbon Reefs within easy reach of Lizard Island.
	OSPREY REEF. 100 kilometres into open ocean. Spectacular drop-offs and visibility.
Best Diving Season	October till late December. Early summer cyclones are uncommon here occurring more frequently further north.
Diving Organisation	Day trips to Cairns and Port Douglas reefs. Snorkelling at Green Island and Low Isles Cay.
	Diving from the resort at Lizard Island.
	Live-aboard diving expeditions north along the Ribbon Reefs to the Cod Hole usually leave from Port Douglas. Special excursions to Osprey Reef.

6. THE NORTHERN REEF AND NORTHERN CORAL SEA

Major Reefs	A ribbon of reefs similar to the Ribbon Reefs proper extends north of Lizard Island for 400 kilometres, then breaks up to form Yule Reef and the Great Detached Reef and Raine Island.
	To the north and east of these are Ashmore, Boot and Portlock Reefs.
Access Ports	All settlement is many hundreds of kilometres away. Cairns, Thursday Island.
Diving Attractions	Very seldom dived.
	Excellent visibility, large pelagic fish schools.
	Sharks.
Best Diving Season	October to mid December
Diving Organisation	Specialist cruises on live-aboard dive vessels

199

ENJOYING THE REEF

Diving on the Great Barrier Reef is the ultimate experience for any diver. Here is some general advice to make that experience as worthwhile and free of trouble as possible.

PREPARATION

Research into a diving destination or holiday pays dividends. For example, make sure that a particular boat trip visits those dive sites that were the reason for choosing the location in the first place. Advice from friends and the growing number of travel agents who specialise in diving holidays is vital. It is now possible to obtain good and reliable advice on the wide range of resorts and boats available. Make use of this resource.

For the photographer, the voltage and configuration of electricity outlets and availability of film and facilities is important. Many dive vessels have both 240 and 110 volt outlets but photographers should take film and back-up equipment.

If you are a qualified diver, make sure that all equipment (including you) is in good shape. Regulator service should be a priority and, if possible, go for a dive before leaving home to make sure that everything works. Non-divers who are intending to do one of the many SCUBA courses available should consult their doctor or, preferably, a doctor with a knowledge of underwater medicine, to ensure that they are medically fit to use SCUBA equipment. Diving is not a dangerous sport, but it does require knowledge and common sense.

The Australian sun shows scant regard for most skin of European origin, so use a sun-screen often and generously and take plenty of back-up supplies.

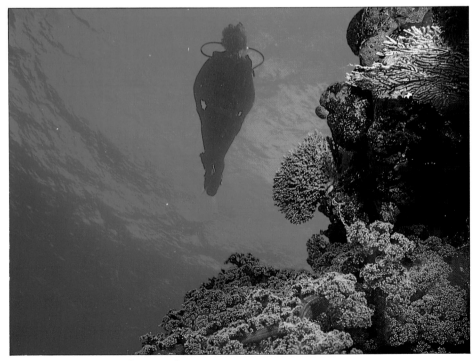

A new explorer enters this soft coral garden.

Underwater photography is complex and demands the right gear. Here wide angle equipment is being used.

DIVING

There is a tendency for divers to make many more dives than usual when they are in exotic locations, so it is wise to dive sensibly and have very conservative dive profiles. A substantial time break during a week of diving is also wise, as decompression sickness is more likely to develop towards the end of a long diving trip.

The currents around many reefs are quite fickle and can vary tremendously in direction and strength even during a short dive. In particular this is experienced at the entrances to reefs and in between reef passages so it is always worthwhile seeking local advice before starting a dive.

During winter and early spring the water can be quite cool, especially in the south. A full wetsuit at least five millimetres thick is generally necessary at this time of year. Likewise, warm clothes are necessary at night. In warmer months, 'long johns' for diving are fine, though protection from marine stingers with a shirt or lycra suit is vital.

WEATHER   Divers are as much attuned to surface conditions as they are to underwater visibility. Seasoned divers will almost always state that the best time to dive on the Great Barrier Reef is from the beginning of October to the end of December. It is then that conditions can be perfect with minimal winds, flat seas and the possibility of days of absolute calm with the sea a pristine surface of silk.

Weather conditions are unpredictable. An early morning dive often provides optimal conditions.

Unfortunately, the only really predictable feature of the weather is its unreliability and even the best planned holiday can run foul of the elements. Likewise, it is possible, though less likely, to enjoy good conditions outside of the most favoured months.

The second half of summer and early autumn is the cyclone season and while conditions may be fine it would be unwise to plan too far in advance for this unsettled time of the year. The cyclone season ends in late April but the heavy rainfall of the preceding few months results in coastal run-off which often severely affects visibility. From May to August persistent large high pressure systems over the centre of the continent of Australia bathe the Barrier Reef area with steady south-easterly winds of ten to twenty knots and one to two metre seas in open waters.

As diving holidays are often planned well in advance, perhaps the best advice for any intending diver is to enjoy perfect conditions to the full, but do not expect them every day. Try and book for mid to late spring or early summer or take pot-luck at other times.

ENJOYMENT

Even though the underwater beauty of the coral reefs is the main attraction, remember that there are plenty of other habitats worth exploring.

The reef flat at low tide is home to many reef animals and the undersides of coral boulders will reveal shells, brittle stars, numerous encrusting sponges and other fascinating organisms. Normal neoprene diving boots with thick soles are generally adequate for walking on reefs, but it is still possible to have a sea-urchin spine penetrate the side of a boot so care should be taken.

Life above the water can add to the thrill of any diving trip. Huge Manta rays may broach the surface of a nearby reef, or a school of porpoises will play games in the wake of the ship. Largest of all, of course, are the humpback whales, found in increasing numbers in Reef waters. These huge creatures arrive in early to mid June from Antarctic waters via the southern Australian coastline, and then migrate northwards. They generally leave Reef waters about October, taking with them their new-born calves.

Inshore water environments, such as the mangrove-covered areas of continental island shores are also fascinating and ideal for snorkelling. However, in the summer months, box-jelly fish, *Cironex fleckeri*, inhabit these areas, so protection with a full wetsuit and hood or lycra suit is essential.

Exploration of the islands themselves, with bird rookeries, turtle hatcheries and a huge variety of vegetation often adds a sense of balance to an expedition. The feel of dry land is usually very welcome after a week at sea.

On the mainland are magnificent rainforests, wild rivers to raft and a host of other experiences. Before, after and between dive trips it is easy to spend a few days enjoying the Queensland coast and hinterland.

Cruising batfish caught in silhouette against the rising sun of a new day.

REEF ETIQUETTE

Divers can experience more of the Reef than any other group of people. As such, they have a responsibility to adopt a preservationist attitude to the marine environment. Dive sites are not unlimited, a fact realised by most dive boat operators who universally frown on the collection of anything unless it is on film.

Be careful when swimming over delicate corals. Plate corals can be much wider than a diver, but are as fragile as egg shells.

Some reefs and corals in specific locations are under scientific study, so obviously any markings or tags must be left undisturbed.

On the reef flat, coral boulders should be returned as soon as possible to their normal positions, to preserve the unique life on all surfaces.

TWO DIVES OF DISTINCTION

THE COD HOLE   The northern extremity of Ribbon Reef Number 10 (150 kilometres north of Port Douglas and almost due east of Lizard Island) is well-protected from the swells of the open ocean. The landward side of this reef is also shielded from any wind-blown swells by a further reef structure.

A special pleasure awaits the diver here. For many years a population of potato cod have made this site a monument to gluttony. Whenever a boat anchors, the fish, some weighing 100 kilograms, are waiting beneath, first to eat any appealing refuse from the boat and then to follow the divers to the reef and consume whatever fish the divers provide. Portly, even corpulent, the cod glide effortlessly from one diver to another anticipating more food. It is possible to be surrounded by two or three massive creatures who nudge divers side on to encourage another dig into the pocket of the buoyancy compensator for yet another offering. It is certainly a novel, and perhaps even an unnerving, experience to swivel around after the departure of one cod and be confronted by the voluminous grin of another literally ten centimetres from the face mask.

A hand stretches out to bridge the gap between the worlds of man and fish.

A remora clings with its modified dorsal fin to the cod. Remora hitch a ride and break off for a snack of left overs from a big fish's meal.

Here at the Cod Hole several fish have found a place where the living is easy. They will always investigate a potential titbit from a diver.

The benevolence of the major players in the drama gives great delight to all visitors here and many smaller fish in the vicinity enter into the spirit of the performance and become much more approachable as well. Two specific character actors deserve a mention. The first is a very large Maori wrasse, which swoops in on the unsuspecting to gulp food and the occasional finger. The diver divests the food and sometimes his hand but may escape totally unharmed.

Moray eels have poor vision but a keen sense of smell and so should be observed closely. At the Cod Hole they often swim quite freely around divers, with their heads foraging into the recesses of a diver's gear. An attack, however, is very unlikely, especially if the diver's movements are slow and deliberate.

Towards the end of the dive, the cod return to the underside of the boat and await the inevitable next meal.

On a rising tide, one of the joys of this location is to drift with the water from the opening between the reefs back towards the cods' usual home territory. Some of the larger cod often join divers and almost seem part of the group, swimming alongside their new human buddies. Photographers and fish alike obtain their rewards.

A cavernous maw? Though a large predator, the potato cod here at the Cod Hole are no serious threat, but should be respected.

The Yongala Wreck

On Thursday 23 March 1911 the pride of the Adelaide Steamship Company's fleet, the *S.S. Yongala*, was last seen on the surface of this planet. On board were 120 passengers and crew, all of whom were to perish in one of Australia's worst peacetime shipwrecks. The *Yongala* took the full fury of a tempest and sank, almost without trace, due east of Cape Bowling Green, 50 nautical miles south of Townsville.

On a calm, clear day the wreck is quite visible from the surface. The uppermost section of the vessel lies in 45 feet of water, while the ship rests on a flat sandy bottom in 100 feet. Due to its position away from the lee of any reefs, however, conditions are seldom flat calm and the only hint as to what lies on the sea floor below may be a surfacing turtle or a bat fish breaking the surface, looking for some breakfast scraps.

Locating the wreck and anchoring onto a buoy on the port side of the *Yongala* will take an hour at the best of times. The distance of the wreck from the shore and the lack of reef so close to the mainland is important to the *Yongala*'s present-day fame. Basically, it is a huge artifical reef with abundant fish and marine life. On every boat before the first dive, there is an air of anticipation and excitement and some mixed emotions about the fate of the sunken vessel, which is considerably larger and seemingly less vulnerable than any dive-boat anchoring to her superstructure.

The underwater spectacle begins at the surface with the sentinel bat-fish escort down the anchor line. The wreck lies on its starboard side, virtually intact, and although it is some 300 feet long, orientation on the vessel is not difficult. Much of the deck structure is no longer present and there are many large bays which are home to a seething mass of various species of pelagic fish.

The fish life is the most staggering aspect of the dive. Schooling fish are present in large numbers and almost unafraid of divers, but the most striking thing is the size of the individuals. They are huge. Almost every fish is one and a half times its normal adult size which is quite extraordinary and at first somewhat unnerving.

A commemorative plaque – to those who lost their lives in the *Yongala*.

Symbols of modernity overcome by time and life; these toilet bowls are now flushed only by the currents.

Like grotesque arms the lifeboat derricks stretch out for boats no longer needed.

The density of fish life is mirrored by the intensity of activity. While observing one activity, there is always something else happening which will demand attention. A sea-snake will swim past; around the stern a school of fish will dissolve away to reveal a 600 pound Queensland grouper; the sunlight will be obliterated by a turtle, or more likely, a huge ray arching over the wreck. The surprises on the first dive are endless and thoroughly intoxicating.

The ship itself is fascinating. Due to its length, usually only half of the ship is tackled on any one dive. A plaque on the hull of the ship serves as remembrance to those who lost their lives in the tragedy. The letters of the name *Yongala* are prominent landmarks at the bow of the vessel and portholes intermingle with a huge variety of sedentary marine life along the ship's length. Clouds of fusilier fish inhabit gangways and cabins and porcelain toilet bowls lie aft of the central dive-boat mooring.

At night the eeriness of the wreck is profound. Many of the pelagic fish disappear and the holes of the ship fill with sleeping wrasse and cod. The odd turtle, frightened by torchlight, swims into the beam of the offending source to seek solace in another part of the vessel. Tubastrea corals inflame the recesses of the archways and caverns of the ship and highlight the *Yongala* experience; a living fireworks display, a celebration of life.

A restless predator, the grey tipped reef shark.

SHARKS

The more remote areas of the Great Barrier Reef and the lesser dived parts of the Coral Sea are world famous for their sharks. It's not that they are absent from other reefs, simply that they have a limited interest in human activities and generally keep clear of divers.

When they are present, the reef sharks tend to swim at a distance from the diver, observing and inquisitive of the huge, bubbling shapes which are new to the territory. Some of the smaller sharks, unsure of the best way to behave, can confront the diver in much the same way as they would another shark when they feel a threat to their territory. Arched movements of the back and forward projection of the teeth in the lower jaw should be enough to convince the diver to move on, which in this situation is the appropriate course of action.

An organised shark feed makes a fascinating dive. Fish caught trawling are arranged along a wire rope and one end is attached to the reef, while the other is attached to a plastic bottle filled with air which suspends the wire vertically.

It does not take long for the sharks to realise the presence of 'free' food and it is not uncommon on some feeds to have ten or more white, black and grey tipped reef sharks surrounding the baits. From an organised orbit, one shark will take a chance and move closer to the bait. One or two more aggressive passes are made and then comes the final move. At impact, the nictitating membranes of the shark's eyes (a protective device) can clearly be seen. There is a sudden thud and then the vibration; the physical sensation of the teeth hitting the fish and the rapid side to side movements of the shark's head as it rips its food from the fish's belly.

After the first shark has attacked the bait, many others move in and the scene often becomes a confused mass of sharks and shreds of fish. A departing shark, dazed from the orgy and oblivious of its surroundings, can veer off towards the surrounding divers.

Often this 'attack' phase lasts for only a few seconds before the sharks back away to observe the scene. Then the wild action will start all over again.

A shark feast requires a fish, a steel trace and then the wait. The bait is set.

The kill is sudden, positive, brutal and final.

FISHING ON THE REEF

CALVIN TILLEY

THERE are more than fifteen hundred different species of fish to be found in the vicinity of the Great Barrier Reef, making it an angler's paradise. However, not all of these are edible or worth catching. They include some of the world's largest and some of the smallest fish, and they range from the most beautiful to the most ugly, and from the best tasting to the most poisonous and toxic.

A small black marlin swims just out of reach of the deckhand's tag pole, while the angler tries to draw it closer.

Fishing in the Great Barrier Reef waters has been taking place for over forty thousand years, since the Aborigines first settled the adjacent coast and islands and dugong and turtle hunting became an important part of their culture. Although white settlement on this part of the coastline started 150 years ago, it has only been in the post-war years that commercial fishing on the Reef commenced in earnest.

In the early years commercial fishing concentrated on Spanish mackerel, which accounted for 90 per cent of fish sales. While mackerel is still the most economically important fin fish taken from the Reef, other species, such as coral trout, sweetlip and red emperor have since become popular and account for a large proportion of the commercial fin fish catch in Queensland.

By far the biggest development in commercial fishing in the area has been prawn fishing. In the early 1960s there were only 300–400 trawlers operating along the coast; today there are approximately 2400 boats. These vessels are far more sophisticated, and therefore efficient, with radars, colour sounders, satellite navigators and electronic course plotters, allowing them to fish in areas where it was previously considered unsafe. The vessels are also powered by diesel engines, with three or four times the horsepower of early vessels, enabling them to pull much larger nets than hitherto.

Technology has not been restricted to the commercial fishing fleet alone. Better boats, more reliable outboards and cheap, reliable radios and sounders have made the Reef more accessible to the ever increasing number of recreational fishermen. It is estimated that more than 600 000 anglers 'wet a line' annually, accounting for about 70 per cent of the fin fish caught on the Reef each year.

The most popular species of fish sought by recreational anglers on the Great Barrier Reef can be divided into two groups, demersal species and pelagic species. Briefly, a demersal fish is one that lives and feeds near the bottom while a pelagic fish is one that lives in the open sea and feeds on or near the surface. Most of the Reef species are demersal fish; coral trout, sweetlip, red emperor, cod, wrasse and tusk fish all belong to this group. The pelagic species are the billfish (marlin and sailfish), mackerel (all four species), trevalley, tuna and numerous other tropical sportfish.

Generally there is no particular fishing season on the Reef so most of the demersal species can be caught all year round. However, it tends to be quieter during the hot summer monsoon. The best period for Reef fishing is considered to be the cooler months from April to November. Because of their open sea nature, fishing for pelagic species seems to be more defined by seasons. They tend to follow the warm ocean currents along the coast and are therefore more prevalent at certain times of the year, although many of them can be found in Reef waters all year round. This is due mainly to the stable water temperature where there is only a change of between five or six degrees from summer to winter. The water is therefore considered 'warm' all year round.

TIME AND TIDE

What many anglers do not realise is that the moon influences the feeding patterns of fish. In each lunar month there are four phases of the moon: the full moon, the last quarter, the new moon, and the first quarter, indicating the moon's position in its orbit around the earth relative to the earth and the sun. The two phases that are of particular interest to anglers are the full moon and the new moon.

The five or six days leading up to the days of the full moon and the new moon are the best periods to fish. This means that in each month there are 12 to 14 days that will fish better than the other 16 to 18 days. It is generally accepted that the best period to fish for demersal species is the five or six days leading up to the full moon. If you check this with a tide chart you will see that it corresponds with the 'making' tides, that is the period when the tides get progressively larger each day.

The optimum period for fishing for pelagics is the five or six days leading up to the new moon. Mackerel, for instance, certainly follow this rule of thumb. Although they can be caught on the making tides leading up to the full moon, mackerel are usually considered to be a dark moon phase fish.

Although all fish can be caught on any day of the month and in any moon phase, the periods mentioned above are those of maximum fish feeding activity. In my experience the best time to fish on any given day is the first few hours as the tide runs in and an hour or so either side of the change in the tide.

SPORT OR REEF FISHING

There are two different fishing techniques used to catch the demersal and pelagic fish; reef or bottom fishing, and sport or game fishing. As implied in the names, reef or bottom fishing is for demersal species such as coral trout, sweetlip, red emperor, cod, etc., while sport or game fishing is for the pelagic species such as mackerel, tuna, trevally, sailfish, marlin, etc.

Reef fishing, as it is commonly known, is popular right along the Queensland coast. Rigs usually comprise a handline of 60–80 pounds breaking point with a large bean sinker of around 4–8 ounces which can slide on the line. Either one or two hooks can then be attached, above or below the sinker. Hook sizes vary from 6/0 to 9/0, with my preference being size 8/0. The most popular baits for reef fishing are fish baits such as mullet or pilchard and squid. The most commonly caught species are from the Serranids (coral trout and cod), Lutjanids(emperor and large or small mouthed nannygai) and the Lethrinids (red throat sweetlip and spangled sweetlip) families. An average day's fishing would normally produce a mixed bag of fish, of perhaps three or four fish up to a dozen or more. The more experienced anglers usually fare better than the novice and it is estimated that only 10 per cent of the anglers catch 40 per cent of the fish.

The distinctive coral trout, *Plectropoma leopardus*, is a demersal fish commonly caught in reef waters.

Sport or game fishing has become progressively more popular over the last 10 years. As the number of boats and anglers increase, individuals have had to become more skilful in order to catch their share of fish. Anglers have realised that you can catch just as many if not more fish using a lighter line and have more fun in the process. Meanwhile modern technology has led to the development of rods and reels of a high standard that may be bought at more affordable prices.

While there is excellent fishing on the extremity of the Reef, it is not necessary to travel that far offshore. Most of the coastal reefs, shoals and islands provide excellent catches for fast moving tropical fish such as Spanish mackerel, trevally, queenfish, barracuda and more. Game fishermen use a variety of techniques to catch their quarry. The common technique is to troll rigged baits or deep diving lures, or a combination

A school of sea perch. The schools may contain several hundred fish and are trawled commercially.

Sweetlips, *Plectorhynchus chaetonoides*, are notoriously shy and shelter close to the coral reef.

of both, along the edge of the reef or rocky outcrop or over the deeper shoals. Drifting whole live or dead fish baits from either an anchored or drifting boat is also a popular method. This can be combined with casting poppers or other surface lures or deep jigs.

These days many anglers have a couple of drifting baits such as a gar or WA pilchard out behind the boat while they are Reef fishing. This rarely fails to produce a Spanish mackerel or two.

For the angler keen to tangle with the high flying acrobatic sailfish or small black marlin it can be as simple as trolling a pattern of rigged baits such as mullet and gar or high speed jet heads and pushers out wide. Both the marlin and sailfish use the giant shallow basin of water between the coast and the Reef as an almost year round home. If you can locate a school of bait out there (usually indicated by the overflying seabirds wheeling and diving) then it is highly likely that the big pelagics will be close by.

A large concentration of these baitfish schools at Cape Bowling Green, near Townsville, has resulted in an unusually high concentration of sailfish and marlin in this area. Catches of up to as many as 10 fish are common, while the record is 16 sailfish and marlin caught by one gameboat in a day.

These days almost all the billfish are tagged and released to live and fight another day.

215

A huge marlin estimated weight 500 kilos (1100 lbs) tries to lift its massive body clear of the water at the back of a gamefishing cruiser at Cairns. This fish was tagged and released as are most of their captures.

FISHING AND THE MARINE PARK

While most of the Great Barrier Reef and adjacent waters are now part of the Great Barrier Reef Marine Park, recreational and commercial activities such as fishing have been catered for. Permits or licences are not required for recreational fishing in Queensland or the Marine Park, however, the zoning system used by the Marine Park Authority for management purposes does restrict or prohibit fishing on some reefs and in some areas. These restrictions enter only a small area of the Marine Park totalling less than 10 per cent.

Copies of the Zoning Plan of the Marine Park are freely available from offices of the Queensland National Parks and Wildlife Service and Great Barrier Reef Marine Park Authority. It is advisable to consult the relevant Zoning Plan before going fishing; it could save you a hefty fine.

A FISHING HOLIDAY

Each year thousands of anglers, Australian and from overseas, visit Queensland on holiday. They have been drawn by the stories of exciting sport fish seemingly just waiting to be caught. Interstate anglers travel to the coast by road with their tackle, and fish their way north. Some tow their boats or even sail them up to the Reef. However, much of the tackle used in southern waters is not suitable for the style of fishing in North Queensland, and it is not always possible to fish anywhere and catch fish.

Many anglers that make the journey to Reef waters find it preferable to book with local fishing tour operators first. There are charter boats available for hire in most major centres along the coast. Every type of fishing is catered for, be it light tackle, game fishing, trolling or spinning, chasing giant black marlin off the edge of the continental shelf or catching sweetlip and coral trout. All bait and tackle is supplied with the charter. If the cost of hire is shared between several anglers it makes this type of fishing much more affordable, and takes a lot of the hit or miss out of fishing. As with any location you can't beat local knowledge, and in this way you are assured of fishing with the right gear in the right place at the right time.

For information on boat charters, tackle, techniques or places to fish, a visit to the local tackle shop is usually worthwhile. Many of the shops along the coast also act as booking agents for charter boats or if not, can advise on the best boat for the type of fishing required and how to contact the owner or skipper.

For anglers wishing to book a charter prior to their trip to the Great Barrier Reef, it usually only requires a visit to a travel agent, since there are many large fishing tour operators who can tailor a fishing holiday to their requirements.

Anyone intending to visit North Queensland to 'wet a line', is advised to try at least one day's charter fishing. Not only will it give you the best chance of catching the fish of a lifetime but it can also be a real education. You might learn a few 'secrets'.

BLACK MARLIN

Portrait of a black marlin. These wild fish attract anglers from all corners of the globe. They offer the ultimate sporting challenge and while the costs are exceptionally high most fishermen consider them worthwhile.

The biggest marlin ever caught in Australian waters. This black marlin weighing 1442 lbs was caught many years back, and is still the Australian record catch on 130 lb test line.

Of all the fish in the oceans none captures the imagination like the giant of the underwater world. There are only four species of fish that grow to one thousand pounds (454 kg) and even fewer that reach two thousand pounds. Of these four, three are members of the billfish family (fish that have a rapier-like sword or bill as an extension of their top jaw), the other a member of the tuna family. They are; the black marlin, the blue marlin, the broadbill swordfish and the Atlantic bluefin tuna.

During the Second World War a young American Officer, George Bransford, was stationed in North Queensland. Impressed by the stories the old fishermen told of huge marlin off the edge of the Reef, he later returned to Cairns, established Bransfords tackle shop and had a game boat built called 'Sea Baby'. A number of big marlin were hooked and lost then in 1966 the first fish over one thousand pounds was landed and weighed. Suddenly Cairns became recognised as the giant black marlin capital of the world.

The largest black marlin landed in Australia so far is a fish of 1442 pounds caught by Cairns angler Mick Magrath in 1973. The reputation of Cairns and, indeed, most of North Queensland as a tourist destination owes much to those early years of gamefishing.

In the early days the fishing was mainly out of Cairns, with the boats returning daily, but over the last fifteen years, as boats travelled further afield, the more prolific grounds to the north of Cairns were discovered. The line of Reefs known as the Ribbons form an almost continuous barrier and it is here that the large fish are most numerous. However, in order to fish this remote area it became necessary for the game boats to have a larger vessel, known as the 'mothership', in attendance for refuelling and to provide accommodation and meals for anglers and crew.

The motherships and their game boats may be at sea for several months at a time, fishing their way north along the ribbons as far as Lizard Island. When a 'hot bite' occurs, the baits get eaten as fast the crew can rig the lines.

Marlin have also been caught off Townsville and the Whitsundays. They move in from the Pacific during the period from late August to December to spawn in the warm waters on the edge of the Great Barrier Reef. The largest black marlin are female, as the male only grows to around 400 pounds. However, a large marlin is not necessarily an old fish; black marlin grow very quickly and a female fish of 1000 pounds may only be eight to ten years old. These fish have no teeth and swallow their food whole. They use their bills to 'whack' another fish, either stunning it long enough for the marlin to swallow it, or even killing it outright.

The favoured technique for catching giant black marlin is to troll whole fish baits such as tuna, mackerel, dolphin fish, rainbow runner and 'scad'. Normally two baits are trolled at a time, with one bait rigged so that it swims (usually a scad) and the other rigged so that it skips across the surface (skip bait is usually a bigger fish such as a tuna or mackerel).

Anglers who have long tackled the powerhouse strength and speed of the black marlin along the Reef have been trying to catch that 2000 pound fish for years. A number have been hooked and lost, some after battles that have lasted an astonishing 24 hours.

The survival of the black marlin as a species depends on their undisturbed spawning off the Great Barrier Reef. Today the majority of marlins that are caught are tagged and released under a government tagging program, and while this continues their future is assured. Perhaps that 2000 pound fish may not be all that far away.

STAYING AND SEEING

CAMILLA SANDELL

T HE Great Barrier Reef stretches for over 2000 kilometres and measures over 70 kilometres at its widest point. It begins near the mouth of New Guinea's Fly River and finishes at Lady Elliot Island, and 98 per cent of that expanse is classified as a Marine Park. That makes it by far the largest Marine Park in the world. Access to such a massive area becomes an important consideration, particularly as the distances between the mainland and the Reef vary widely. At some points the Reef is a mere 20 kilometres from the mainland; at others it can be as distant as 150 kilometres. There is nowhere, despite what some people may think, where you can simply walk into the water and stumble across the Reef.

When deciding how to see the Reef you have numerous choices. You can arrange a package holiday and have your holiday planned from the beginning, or you can plan very little and take one day at a time. Obviously, sometimes bookings will be required, particularly during peak season. Many of the jumping-off points for the Barrier Reef can be reached by plane, rail and coach from various locations around Australia. Accommodation can be found on the mainland, at an island resort or on a cruise boat or a dive charter boat. The wide range available means that all budgets can be catered for.

GETTING THERE

Ansett and Australian Airlines offer flights from all major Australian cities to various Queensland destinations. Other airlines operating services include East-West, Air New South Wales, Noosa Air, Air Queensland, Sunstate Airlines. See entries under individual resorts and towns for more specific information.

The distances involved in travelling within Australia can make coach trips a little like endurance tests, but they are certainly one of the cheapest ways of getting around. The companies operating services from major cities include Ansett Pioneer, Greyhound, McCafferty's, Deluxe Coachlines, AAT and Olympic East West Express.

Trains to destinations in Queensland can be taken from all major cities. Check with a travel agent or local train station for further information.

Package holidays can be arranged through your travel agent.

THE ISLANDS

LADY ELLIOT ISLAND

Lady Elliott is 80 kilometres northeast of Bundaberg, and can be reached daily from there by light aircraft. Flights are also available from Brisbane.

Lady Elliot is the southernmost island of the Great Barrier Reef, named by Captain Stewart in 1816 after his ship, the *Lady Elliot*. It has a wide selection of accommodation, from safari tents pitched amongst pisonia trees to cabins with private facilities. Lady Elliot's attractions are geared towards divers and snorkellers, photographers and nature lovers.

The island's aquarium boasts a 'Creature Feature'. This programme is aimed at familiarising visitors with some of the marine animals and fish of the Reef, which are exhibited for a period of only 24 hours each before being returned to their natural habitat.

Lady Elliot has a fully-equipped dive shop, where equipment can be hired. Diving instruction to Open Water Diving Certificate can be arranged over five days. Shore-entry dives, off-shore dives, underwater dive trails and night diving are all available.

Turtles nest here and the island has vast rookeries of nesting seabirds.

Lady Elliot Island.

HERON ISLAND

Heron is only 72 kilometres from Gladstone and access is by helicopter or a one-and-a-half hour sea-trip by catamaran.

Heron is one of only three islands actually located on the Reef itself. It sits mere metres above the coral, making it an extremely popular resort for divers, who flock to enjoy a wide diversity of dives, excellent visibility and ideal temperatures, as well as those more interested in less active holiday pursuits. Heron caters for a large and varied range of people of all ages and is equipped with up-to-date facilities. Reef-walking, conducted walks, informative talks and forays in semi-submersibles are some of the island's more popular activities.

THE WHITSUNDAY ISLANDS

These include Hamilton, Hayman, Daydream, Lindeman, Brampton, Long and South Molle, all of which lie somewhere between 25 and 80 kilometres from the Reef. They are 'continental' islands, which means that they are actually land masses rather than coral cays. In their surrounding waters, warm and rich in nutrients, both hard and soft coral flourishes.

The Whitsunday Passage is the body of water between the 74 islands and the Queensland coast, and an area which has become increasingly popular with tourists. Known for its beauty as well as its safe waters, many tourists opt for the Whitsunday Passage as their destination. They charter their own yachts and explore the Reef and its islands with a great degree of freedom. Most of the yacht charter companies are based in Shute Harbour and Airlie Beach, and hire out bareboat or fully-crewed yachts.

The two major mainland resorts of the Whitsunday Coast are Airlie Beach and Shute Harbour, both of which are major jumping-off points for the Whitsunday Islands.

BRAMPTON ISLAND

Brampton is 32 kilometres north-west of Mackay. It is a mountainous island with lush forests, palm trees, a coconut grove and white sandy beaches. Brampton is a particularly popular destination for those wishing to make a day trip from Mackay.

LINDEMAN ISLAND

Lindeman Island lies at the southern entrance to the Whitsunday Passage. Settled in 1906 as a grazing lease it was the first island resort in the Whitsundays.

The resort was completely rebuilt in 1987 and now offers a nine hole golf course, 150 rooms, two restaurants, tennis courts and seven secluded sandy beaches. Ninety per cent of the island is National Park. Excellent walking tracks lead to all parts of the island including Mt. Oldfield, the highest point. Here you can view almost all of the Whitsunday Islands in one breathtaking sweep.

HAMILTON ISLAND

Hamilton is the island which has become the focal point of the Whitsunday group and often serves as a base from which to explore the other islands. Located in the heart of the Whitsunday group, Hamilton comprises a new resort and a 30-hectare fauna park with a wide variety of Australian fauna.

Hamilton's airport receives several daily flights from Sydney and Brisbane. The range of accommodation and tourist facilities is extensive. A 'Coral Cat' transports the island's visitors, divers and snorkellers to a large platform anchored on the coral from which they can see and explore the Reef. Moored at the platform is a glass-sided submarine used for underwater viewing.

LONG ISLAND

Long Island lies 8 kilometres south-east of Shute Harbour. Its two resorts, Happy Bay and Palm Bay, are located at the northern end of the island, and are both quiet and secluded. The island is studded with casuarinas and coconut palms.

SOUTH MOLLE ISLAND

Lying in the heart of the Whitsunday Passage, South Molle Island is just 8 kilometres from Shute Harbour. It comprises over 400 hectares of National Park with excellent walking tracks and panoramic views over the islands.

Brampton Island.

HAYMAN ISLAND

This resort prides itself upon being 'the jewel of the Whitsundays . . . created with a flawless sense of style and sophistication.' Recent projects have seen the development of a world class island resort, set amongst 13 hectares of rainforest and surrounded by two white sandy beaches and a man-made lagoon. The philosophy of 'only the best' is reflected in a high standard of elegantly furnished and beautifully appointed accommodation, a stunning freshwater and saltwater swimming pool complex, a choice of six restaurants and extensive evening entertainment. Recreation and sporting amenities include: daily trips to the Great Barrier Reef; parasailing; waterskiing; sailboarding; yacht charter; fishing; helicopter and amphibian trips; secluded picnics; day and night tennis; aqua aerobics; bushwalking; badminton; gymnasium and health centre. Other guest facilities range from a Children's Activity Centre to florists and beauticians.

Access to Hayman, the most northerly of the Whitsunday group, is usually via Hamilton Airport, where visitors are welcomed aboard the luxurious *Sun Goddess* or *Sun Paradise* for the short trip north to Hayman. Hayman's diving base is the *Reef Goddess*, an 18 metre cruiser crewed by fully-qualified diving instructors who teach daily from Bait Reef, 40 minutes from Hayman.

Hayman Island – the 'jewel' of the Whitsundays.

DAYDREAM ISLAND

Just 5 kilometres from Shute Harbour, Daydream Island can be reached by launch (20 minutes), departing several times daily or by water taxi (40 minutes). It is the smallest island resort in the Whitsunday group, at only 38 acres. The island has many natural attractions being partly covered by subtropical rainforest and Norfolk Pines, with fringing coral reefs located at its northern end.

The current resort caters for up to 200 guests and offers all-inclusive holiday packages. It boasts one of the largest free-formed salt water pools in the southern hemisphere.

The resort closed in mid 1989 for extensive redevelopment. The new 300-room, four star resort, due to be completed in early 1991, will be the second largest island resort on the Great Barrier Reef. It will offer a high standard of accommodation, a marina and a unique day visitor theme park located separately at the southern end of the island. Extensive landscaping will be carried out to enhance the island's natural environment.

Daydream Island.

NEWRY ISLAND

Access to Newry is from Victor Creek. The island is 56 kilometres north of Mackay, and boasts excellent fishing and an abundant supply of oysters, a koala sanctuary and a relaxed and unpretentious atmosphere.

MAGNETIC ISLAND

Magnetic Island is only 8 kilometres from Townsville, and there are a variety of ways of traversing that distance. Magnetic is serviced by fast catamaran and helicopter, a regular ferry service or a car can be taken onto the island by vehicular ferry.

Magnetic is a mountainous island, and about half of its 5148 hectares is classified as National Park. Twenty-four kilometres of walking track wind through bushland that is home to a variety of vegetation. The wildlife that can be spotted includes koalas, rock wallabies, brush-tailed possums and many species of birds. Magnetic Island, with its secluded bays, palm trees, tropical beaches and rocky headlands, has over 2300 permanent residents. There is also a camping reserve.

HINCHINBROOK ISLAND

Hinchinbrook is 22 kilometres from the coastal town of Cardwell, the departure point for the *Reef Venture*, the 28-foot Power Cat that transports visitors to the island (Tuesday to Sunday inclusive). Alternatively, a seaplane departs Cairns (Wednesday and Saturday) and Townsville (Monday, Wednesday, Friday, Saturday and Sunday) for Hinchinbrook Island.

The resort occupies one small tip of Hinchinbrook, the world's largest island National Park with possibly the world's smallest population — the resort accommodates a maximum of 30 visitors. The island is 52 kilometres long and 1 kilometre wide, and has 11 sandy beaches, rainforests, bush walks and Queensland's third highest mountain, Mt. Bowen. Wildlife includes wallabies, goannas, echidnas and around 250 species of birds. Cruises can be taken to other parts of the island. These take in Hinchinbrook's magnificent mangroved estuary and a beautiful 100-metre waterfall.

ORPHEUS ISLAND

Located some 80 kilometres northeast of Townsville and 24 kilometres offshore, Orpheus is one of the few remaining privately owned islands. The resort is relaxed and exclusive, catering for a maximum of 50 guests and offering complete escapism amidst its 1398 hectare National Park with seven sandy beaches.

Orpheus is popular with serious fishermen and also with those interested in coral gazing. Of the 350 varieties of coral which have been identified within the Great Barrier Reef, 340 can be found in the waters off Orpheus. Facilities include snorkelling, windsurfers, paddleboards, catamarans and outboard dinghies (in which you can take sumptuous picnics to the beach of your choice). Scuba diving, water skiing, sports fishing and cruising charters aboard the highspeed Power Cat can also be arranged.

Transfers to Orpheus are by Air Whitsunday's seaplane service from Townsville. Helicopter and launch services are also available for private charter.

Orpheus Island.

Bedarra Bay resort, Bedarra Island

BEDARRA ISLAND

Bedarra lies 124 kilometres south of Cairns, and is home to two exclusive resorts — Bedarra Bay and Bedarra Hideaway. Its features are fairly typical of many of the Reef islands. The island has beautiful white sandy beaches, secluded bays and lush vegetation.

DUNK ISLAND

By air from Townsville or Cairns, by launch from Clump Point or by water taxi, Dunk is a fairly accessible island. Mostly National Park, Dunk is a tropical island featuring rainforest and secluded sandy beaches, 13 kilometres of walking track and an area set aside for campers. The island boasts an artists' colony, a dairy farm, only one 142-room resort and day cruises through the Family Group of Islands.

FITZROY ISLAND

Fitzroy is a 880 hectare continental island 320 hectares of which are lush tropical rainforest. Almost completely surrounded by coral reef, the calm waters of the bay provide a deep natural anchorage making the island a favourite spot for boating, diving and fishing enthusiasts.

Aside from the abundance of living coral to be seen from Fitzroy, the island also features a Visitors' Centre with a 30-metre freshwater swimming pool, bar and landscaped garden, a range of accommodation from beach house bungalows to comfortable villas, a mini supermarket, a fully equipped dive shop and beach hire facilities. Fitzroy is the only island where a semi-submersible is available to view the array of coral without visiting the outer Barrier Reef. Extension cruise to Moore Outer Reef leaves from Fitzroy Island.

Fitzroy can be reached easily by a 50-minute cruise in a high-speed catamaran. These are run by Great Adventures Cruises, and leave from their Cairns terminal daily. Coach pick-up from hotels can be arranged.

GREEN ISLAND

A true coral cay, Green Island has lush rainforest, with white sandy beaches surrounded by vast coral gardens. It is classified as National Park.

This beautiful island is ideal for snorkelling, swimming and glass-bottomed boat viewing of the Reef. The world's first underwater observatory gives a remarkable view of marine life.

Luxurious catamarans and launches depart daily from Cairns, and it is a 45 minute cruise to Green Island. Coach pick-up from hotels can be arranged.

MICHAELMAS CAY

Michaelmas Cay is a tiny coral island on the outer Reef, northeast of Cairns. Known as 'the isle of birds', it has one of the largest seabird rookeries in the southern hemisphere. Access is restricted to protect the birds.

The island is a National Park and is surrounded by coral reefs. It is ideal for snorkelling, scuba-diving, and viewing the marine life from a glass-bottomed boat or semi-submersible coral viewer.

Daily cruises depart from Cairns and coach pick-ups from hotels are available.

LOW ISLES

This island is surrounded by coral gardens and inhabited only by lighthouse keepers. It can be reached by fast catamaran, and the trip includes the use of glass-bottomed boats and snorkelling gear, the advice of a snorkelling adviser, a guided beach walk with a marine biologist and reef-walking at low tide.

LIZARD ISLAND

Lizard, a 90-minute flight from Cairns, is the island from which James Cook fled the Barrier Reef after the *Endeavour* stuck fast to the Reef in August 1770. Lizard has room for relatively few guests and is an exclusive resort, with excellent cuisine and a variety of activities including watersports, bushwalking in the National Park and tennis. Numbers are swelled by the numerous boat-based fishermen and divers attracted to the waters off the island by the game fishing, the enormous potato cod and the moray eels.

Lizard Island.

Green Island.

TO THE OUTER REEF

MOORE REEF FROM CAIRNS

Moore Reef is 25 kilometres east of Fitzroy Island and 40 minutes from Cairns. It is a large reef and close to the outer edge of the Great Barrier Reef, consisting of eight kilometres of horseshoe shaped reef and staghorn coral.

The newly constructed 20-metre pontoon features a totally shaded area, new seating, showers and changing rooms. Snorkelling gear, glass-bottomed boats and a buffet luncheon are included in the tour price.

Passengers can cruise direct to the reef or via Fitzroy Island for a two-hour stopover. Cruises depart from the Great Adventures terminal, Cairns and pick-up from hotels is available.

NORMAN REEF FROM CAIRNS

The cruise departs from Cairns and goes either direct or with a two-hour stopover on Green Island to the Reef. Pick-ups from hotels can be arranged.

Norman Reef's coral crevasses and gardens are some of the best in the world. Passengers can discover rainbow-coloured coral, multi-striped fish and giant clams on the semi-submersible coral viewer and glass-bottomed boats. Snorkelling equipment is provided and a marine expert offers guided snorkelling tours.

The 45-metre pontoon is equipped with barbecue facilities and there is an underwater observatory where fish are fed half hourly.

AGINCOURT REEF FROM PORT DOUGLAS

The Quicksilver catamaran departs Port Douglas daily and arrives at one of the most spectacular sections of the Reef after a 90-minute cruise. There is a variety of ways to see the vast coral cliffs and gardens. Snorkelling gear is provided free and a marine biologist offers guided snorkelling tours. A 10-metre tender takes accredited divers to two dive sites. The mooring platform contains the outer reef's only underwater observatory, and two semi-submersibles with windows just below sea level make coral viewing trips. Visitors without cars may arrange coach pick-up in Cairns.

DIVING

Full qualifications are needed before someone can teach diving skills. Ensure that your school instructor has qualifications recognised by one of the following organisations: PADI (Professional Association of Diving Instructors), NAUI (National Association of Underwater Instructors), FAUI (Federation of Australian Underwater Instructors).

There are many diving schools in the holiday resorts offering abbreviated 'resort courses' of instruction including a dive or two in Reef waters. They do not give the pupil any qualifications, but are designed really to get people into the water and enjoying the Reef as quickly and safely as possible. Some people do use their trips to the Reef to complete full diving qualifications.

The keenest divers generally choose to join a specialist dive charter boat. They can either charter a whole boat, as a group or club for example, or they can simply book a place on one of the scheduled diving programmes.

Most dive trips take between six and 12 days, but weekend and overnight excursions can be arranged. Charter costs include all meals, accommodation, all or some diving equipment and unlimited airfills. Most boats provide their own divemaster.

CRUISING AND SAILING

Although the Great Barrier Reef has claimed many an unwary vessel as its victim, one of the most idyllic ways to see and enjoy the Reef is to spend a day or more cruising its waters. There are numerous companies that offer craft of all shapes and sizes — to cater for all tastes.

CRUISING HOLIDAYS

Luxurious cruisers such as Coral Princess Cruises (based at Townsville), Roylen Cruises (based at Mackay Harbour) and the Coral Cat (from Hamilton Island) visit various island resorts and deserted coral cays as well as the Outer Reef itself. In the Whitsundays, romantic sailing and camping adventures are offered by the Cygnus, a 55-foot ketch, or the Golden Plover, a 100-foot brigantine built in Melbourne in 1910. You can choose between tall ships, elegant yachts and catamarans or motor cruisers: even the most inexperienced can learn boating skills and enjoy a relaxing holiday in the hands of an expert crew.

FISHING SAFARIS

Three or five day trips are available, combining the challenge of game fishing and reef fishing — as well as the opportunity to enjoy swimming and snorkelling and then disembark on an island for evening entertainment. Boats are professionally crewed and carry all fishing equipment; expert advice and instruction is available.

PLAIN SAILING

Bareboat charters are the cheapest and most basic form of yacht charter: the client hires the yacht of his choice and brings his own food and drink. The yacht comes equipped with cooking equipment, linen, blankets, pillows, fishing and snorkelling gear, dinghy with outboard, navigational equipment, charts and fuel (full tank). Extras may include a sailboard, scuba equipment, provisioning service, cook and/ or skipper. Yacht charter companies offer varying sizes and types of yachts (and varying equipment). Instruction is available for novices. Any damage is covered either by security bond or by insurance.

Most yacht charter companies encourage sailing around the relatively safe waters of the Whitsunday Passage and are based in this area.

Options include Australian Bareboat Charters, Cumberland Charter Yachts, Hamilton Island Charters, Mandalay Boat Charters, Queensland Yacht Charters and Whitsunday Rent-a-Yacht.

Chartering a yacht through one of the many bareboat charter companies is a popular way of holidaying on the Reef.

MAINLAND RESORTS

In recent years staying on the mainland has become a more popular alternative for those interested in seeing the Reef, largely because there has been quite an improvement in the facilities available. There is also the added advantage of being able to travel easily in the other direction — into varied landscape that is Queensland's interior.

All the major towns from Bundaberg in the south to Port Douglas in the north have regular daily cruise departures, with Shute Harbour, Townsville and Cairns being the most popular points of embarkation. Not all of these will visit the Reef proper because of the distances involved, but will instead cruise the waters around the inner islands. Most mainland resorts, including the three major ones mentioned, have an enormous variety of accommodation, ranging from top-class international hotels to the typical Australian-style motels. Those on a limited budget can find affordable accommodation such as 'backpackers' hostels and camping is possible in many places along the coast.

Those with a limited amount of time may find staying on the mainland much more convenient. From Cairns, Port Douglas and Townsville overnight weekend cruises and dive trips can be taken. From Cairns and Townsville fast day cruise boats allow visitors to see at least some of the Reef proper in only a day. For those with an even tighter schedule Air Whitsunday provides a four-seater Buccaneer amphibian for charter. This is also a day trip, departing from Airlie Beach for Hardy Lagoon on the Great Barrier Reef. Not only does it provide a way of seeing the magnificent Whitsunday Islands, but also allows time for reef-walking and snorkelling in Hardy Lagoon.

Ansett, Australian Airlines, the Queensland Government Tourist Bureau and many independent tour operators have an extensive variety of mainland-based and island resort programmes, including combination holidays on the Great Barrier Reef and Queensland hinterland.

BUNDABERG

This is one of the major cities on Queensland's Sugar Coast, and, as well as being only 80 kilometres from Lady Elliot Island, boasts some interesting tourist attractions.

It is the site of the Millaquin Sugar Company, the only mill in Australia which processes sugar from the raw right through to power alcohol and rum. Bundaberg is also close to several beaches, some less than half an hour's drive from the town. Some of the attractions of Bundaberg's surrounding coastline are the fishing, the environment park which is one of the few breeding grounds for sea turtles on the mainland, the surfing and the swimming.

ROCKHAMPTON

With excellent air, rail and coach connections, Rockhampton is the natural jumping off point for Reef islands such as Great Keppel, Heron and Lady Musgrave.

MACKAY

A major departure point for the Great Barrier Reef and island resorts, such as Newry and Brampton Island. Mackay is connected by air with major southern ports.

SHUTE HARBOUR AND AIRLIE BEACH

These are busy resorts at the northern end of Conway National Park, and here are located various departure points for motor cruises and sailing vessels bound for the islands and the Whitsunday Passage. From here you can take day trips to resort islands, sailing cruises to uninhabited islands, fishing cruises and diving excursions. There are a number of mainland activities in the area — coach tours, moke hire, bushwalks, beachcombing and trail riding are some of them. There are also the famous toad races at Airlie Beach Hotel on Tuesdays and Thursdays.

CONWAY NATIONAL PARK

This is Queensland's largest coastal National Park and forms the western and mainland edge of the Whitsunday Passage and islands. Within it there are limited walking tracks and camping and picnic facilities.

TOWNSVILLE

Founded in 1864 Townsville first became a tourist destination at the turn of the century when steamships and sailing boats would make their last stop there before setting off overseas. Many of the grand hotels of this era remain. The Port of Townsville is now an important export outlet for the surrounding resource-rich region of Australia. Townsville is the site of the James Cook University of North Queensland, the Australian Institute of Marine Science and the CSIRO Tropical Agricultural Research Station — as well as the Great Barrier Reef Marine Park Authority. It is also home to many tourist organisations and offers easy access to islands such as Magnetic, Hinchinbrook and Orpheus. The Great Barrier Reef Wonderland, opened in 1987, features the world's largest live coral aquarium, the first Omnimax Theatre in the southern hemisphere and a branch of the Queensland Museum.

CAIRNS

This city has seen phenomenal growth in recent years largely through its international airport which gives easy access for those who want to make the Great Barrier Reef their first — or only — port of call. Located on the shore of Trinity Inlet, the city is characterised by a mixture of traditional and modern architecture and by its relaxed and friendly atmosphere. It offers an enormous variety of accommodation and excellent shopping and tourist facilities. Cairns is the gateway to the tropical wilderness of the Cape York Peninsula, the huge areas of sugar cane fields on the coast, the fertile farming country of the Atherton Tablelands, the rainforests of the Daintree National Park — and to the Great Barrier Reef.

Cairns.

USEFUL INFORMATION

Queensland Government Tourist Bureaux are located in all major cities in Australia, and there are overseas offices in London, Los Angeles, New Zealand, Tokyo and Munich.

The Australian Tourist Commission also has overseas offices in London, Los Angeles, Tokyo, Frankfurt, New Zealand, New York, Toronto.

For more information on the Great Barrier Reef Marine Park contact:

The Great Barrier Reef Marine Park Authority, the
National Parks and Wildlife Service, or the
Wonderland Office, all in Townsville.

If you intend to camp on any of the islands you will require a camping permit.

Glossary

ahermatypic: corals which lack symbiotic algae, the zooxanthellae.

algae: non-vascular or simple green plants.

aragonite: calcium carbonate formed in coral skeleton.

ascidian: class of lower chordate animals which are solitary or colonial and remain permanently attached to the sea floor. They feed by filtering sea water which is continually drawn through their bodies.

atolls: coral islands and reefs surrounding a central lagoon.

autotrophs: organisms able to synthesise nutrients from non-living precursors, e.g. many bacteria and green plants.

axial: the axis in the central core of an organism, e.g. the axial polyp in *Acropora* corals is the one at the centre of the growing tip of a branch.

baleen: horny plates made of fused hair within the mouths of baleen whales, used to filter the whales' food.

beachrock: sand and coral particles which, under the influence of sun and water, fuse together to form a soft rock. Found predominantly on the windward side of cays.

benthic: animals and plants living in or on the sea bottom.

bioerosion: break down of rock or similar substance by biological forces such as boring by snails or dissolving from animal or plant secretions.

bivalves: class of the phylum Mollusca in which the shell is formed in two parts, i.e. two valves.

bommie: large and discrete coral formation.

bryozoans: phylum of animals which resemble corals in having a colonial habit of secreting a skeleton, but are much more complex. Colonies are generally small and delicate. Also called lace corals.

caecum: caeca are blind sacs which project from some cavity, e.g. the human appendix is a caecum from the gut.

calcareous: made from calcium salts, in particular calcium carbonate or limestone.

cays: islands formed by accumulated sand and rubble on top of a coral reef.

cephalopods: class of the phylum Mollusca in which the shell is usually reduced or absent and the foot is modified into a number of suckered tentacles. Examples are squid and octopus.

chordates: major phylum of animals which possess a notochord, i.e. a rod of large vaculated cells in a firm sheath living below the spinal tube. Most are also vertebrates (fish, reptiles, birds and mammals) having a backbone.

ciguatera: a disease caused by eating fish in which a toxin derived from planktonic plants has accumulated.

coelenterates: a general term for animals such as anemones, corals and jellyfish.

continental islands: islands created by the submergence of land all about them, i.e. the peaks remaining after inundation of the coastal plain.

continental shelf: shallow seas (less than 200 metres deep) found around continents.

coprophagy: feeding upon faeces.

corallite: individual skeletal cup which supports a coral polyp.

coral polyp: individual coral organism with a single mouth and set of tentacles. Most corals are colonial and made up of numerous attached polyps.

crustacean: phylum of animals with jointed legs and hard skeleton. Examples are crabs and prawns.

cuvierian tubules: long sticky threads extruded from the cloaca (anus) of some sea cucumbers as a defence mechanism.

deltaic system: a system of branching channels, as at the mouth of a river.

detritovores: animals which feed upon detritus.

detritus: dead plant or animal material, which is broken into small pieces and is covered with microbes (bacteria, fungi, protogoans).

echinoderms: phylum of animals characterised by possessing calcareous plates in their skin, being pentaradial (five armed) and having a water vascular system, e.g. starfish, sea urchins, sea cucumbers.

ecosystem: plants, animals and other organisms which live and interact with each other and with their habitat.

El Nino effect: every three to five years the surface waters of the central and eastern Pacific Ocean become unusually warm at the Equator. These events are called El Ninos and apart from disturbing marine life are thought to cause flooding or drought in other parts of the globe.

fringing reef: reef system around the edges of the mainland or mainland islands.

fronds: leaf-like branches.

gametes: sex products, i.e. sperm and eggs.

gastropod: class of molluscs characteristically having a single whorled shell which encloses the body.

guano: faeces of sea birds, rich in phosphates, which accumulate at roost sites.

hermaphrodite: having functional sex organs of both male and female simultaneously.

hermatypic: corals which possess zooxanthellae, the symbiotic algae, within their tissues.

heterotrophs: organisms which are unable to synthesise nutrients from inorganic sources, but require organic food, e.g. animals.

hydroids: class of cnidarians (coelenterates) with mainly frond-like colonies and which show alternation of generations from sedentary asexual colonies to planktonic sexual medusae (i.e. jellyfish).

invertebrates: animals without a backbone.

macroalgae: large algae, i.e. seaweeds.

microatolls: coral colonies growing on a reef flat which are prevented from growing up by the sea level, but which continue to grow around the edges. The centre often dies.

microbes: general term for much microscopic life, such as bacteria, fungi and protozoans.

microborers: small organisms which bore holes in coral and rock and other hard surfaces such as mollusc shells.

microclimate: special climatic characters (temperature, oxygen levels etc.) which occur very close to the surface or within some tiny cavity.

nektonic: swimming freely in the water, e.g. fish.

nematocyst: stinging cell found in all cnidarians (corals, anemones, jellyfish) consisting of a vacuole and an extrusive thread.

parthogenetic: able to reproduce without the need for fertilisation from a male.

pedicellariae: small defensive and cleaning organelles with pincer-like valves found on the surface of some echinoderms, e.g. sea urchins.

photosynthesis: ability to make sugars and thus food energy from inorganic materials (carbon dioxide and water) and sunlight.

phytoplankters: plant members of the plankton.

planktivores: animals which feed on plankton.

plankton: organisms which float or drift in the water spending all or part of their lives adapted to this mode of living.

planula: larval stage of corals.

platform/patch reef: corals grow to form reefs. The gross shape of the reef may be described as a platform — growing out horizontally, or a patch — growing isolated from nearby reefs.

pneumatophores: specialised structures on the roots of some mangroves which grow up into the air to allow the tree to absorb oxygen unavailable in mangrove muds.

polymorphic life cycles: life cycles with several stages, e.g. caterpillars, pupae, moths.

polyps: *see* coral polyp.

protozoans: several groups (phyla) of single celled animals such as ciliates or amoebae.

ribbon reef: long narrow reefs, largely north-south orientated, which form a more or less continuous ribbon-like barrier.

rugose coral: corals with a wrinkled or ridged appearance.

scleractinian coral: corals of the order Scleractinia, i.e. predominantly the reef building corals but excluding a few such as organ-pipe coral and fire coral.

septum: septa are partitions, especially skeletal plates in the corallite or cup in which the coral polyp lives.

sessile animals: those animals which live attached to the sea bed or to some substrate, e.g. corals and sponges.

siphonophores: specialised order of colonial hydroids which live a planktonic life and in which one or more members may be adapted to float, e.g. Portuguese man-o'-war.

spicules: small particles, usually of calcium carbonate, embedded in soft tissue and which provide support or protection.

stolon: creeping stem or runner from which new individuals may arise.

substrate: a surface, e.g. rock, sand, mud, mollusc shell, mangrove root.

symbiont: organism which lives in a more or less permanent association with another.

symbiosis: a general term for living together in a more or less permanent association, e.g. parasites and host, mutuals which are physiologically interdependent.

Tethys Sea: more than 65 million years ago this large seaway separated Europe and Africa and continued eastwards across southern Asia, north of the Indian shield.

trepang: dried and smoked sea cucumbers — a culinary delicacy, especially in China. Also known as bêche-de-mer.

wall reef: reef rising vertically from considerable depth.

zoanthid: small groups of anemone-like coelenterates.

zooplankton: animal members of the plankton.

zooxanthellae: symbiotic algae which live permanently within the tissues of many corals, some clams and other animals and which, by their ability to photosynthesise, greatly assist in the metabolism of the host. They especially aid the deposition of calcium for the skeleton.

INDEX